Hope this gi...
Coughs

TALES FROM A WANDERING MIND

GILLIAN NEWBERRY

Copyright © 2017 by Gillian Newberry
All photographs and drawings © Gillian Newberry

All rights reserved. This book or any portion thereof may not be reproduced or used in any manner whatsoever without the express written permission of the publisher except for the use of brief quotations in a book review.

Printed by CreateSpace, An Amazon.com Company
Printed in the United States of America

Published by the author, Gillian Newberry, Spartanburg, South Carolina

ISBN-13:   978- 1976078859
ISBN-10:   1976078857

Book and cover design by Janie Marlow, webmaster@namethatplant.net

Introduction

OVER THE YEARS I have given many lectures, talks, and field trips. To keep my audience interested, I have interspersed anecdotes and stories into the presentations. Many people have said laughingly, "You ought to write a book."

Upon retiring after teaching botany for forty years at a small university in the botanical wonderland of upper South Carolina, I was still getting the same prompts.

I'm not special, but special things keep happening to me. Many of these are humorous.

As I looked back on the foibles of my teaching career, I pondered the possible. Maybe I *should* write a book. But I can't spell, and punctuation such as commas, colons, and semicolons are hieroglyphics to me.

But to quiet the voices, I have made an honest attempt. Many people have assisted me in this endeavor. I have ruined the spelling of at least two proofreaders. Without the encouragement and support of all these vocal people, this book would still be an "ought to" instead of "I really did it!"

Some names have been altered and some have been retained; if you recognize yourself please consider it a compliment.

Table of Contents

Home

A Nude in the Attic 9
Wicked Wilma 14
The Mud Dauber and the Puritan Ethic 18
Aqueous Humor...................... 22
I Was Not Meant to Be a Mother 26
A Saturday in August.................... 31
My New Housemate 36
The Taurus and the Bull 39
A Thanksgiving for Three 43
The Unknown Keeps On Giving................ 46
The Sweet Scent of Home 48
The Study 51
The Budgie (Parakeet) with No Language 53
It's the Law........................ 54
Well, It's Happening 57

Hound Tales

Fleabags 60
An End and a Beginning *or*
    The Changing of the Guards 64
A Dog with an Alias 69
Symbiosis 73
The Dog No One Wanted 75
Dodge 78
Is He Dead Yet?..................... 82

Tales and Trails of a Botany Professor

- There Is Safety in Numbers 86
- Cows and Nettles 90
- An Invigorating Experience 92
- A Terminal Addiction 96
- Out of the Jaws of a Cow...................... 99
- I'm Not Going to Tell My Mother............... 103
- Mind Over Metal 112
- The Mud Puppy and the Bride 115
- E-I-E-I-O................................... 118
- I Still Remember 120
- The Perfect Student 122
- Excuses, Excuses 123
- Hoping Is Coping............................ 127

Ponderings

- Reflections 130
- The Ides.................................... 132
- The Best Part of the Day 134
- Southern Greens 136
- The Murmuring Pines and the Hemlocks........ 138
- The Saming of the South..................... 140
- Cycles of Change 143
- Thoughts on a Sunday Afternoon 145
- The Drought................................ 147
- A Trace of Rain.............................. 149
- BASEBALL 150
- Ode to a Tomato Sandwich.................... 152
- Comfort Food 154
- The Dilemma Facing Middle America........... 156
- My Mother's Hand........................... 162
- The Doc in the Box.......................... 163

Postscript 165

List of Plates 167

HOME

A Nude in the Attic

AUGUST IN UPSTATE SOUTH CAROLINA is like the Sahara without sand. The temperature rises into the high 90's for weeks on end and plummets into the low 80's at night. The air is saturated with water, and the dew point is rarely lower than 70. All the clichés for "It's so hot that a (fill in the blank)" apply.

The Southerner's body is slowly acclimatized to this fierce heat throughout the long spring. May offers days in the low 80's and 50's at night. In June the daytime temperatures are in the high 80's, and they dip to 60's in the evenings. In July the highs are in the 90's, with lows hovering in the 70's. And then comes August. August just sits down and pushes. Rain only comes in brief thunderstorms or when a hurricane skirts the coast. It rains just enough to saturate the air with water vapor.

Most transplants from the North arrive in South Carolina in the summer with internal thermostats set for the brief summers of Maine.

This is what happened to me. I finished my PhD in Wisconsin in July of 1976 and accepted a teaching position at a small public liberal arts college in western South Carolina. The transfer did not go smoothly. My worldly goods had to be stored when I arrived, as I had no place to stay. One of my new colleagues offered my dog Coco and me a place on his couch. Every day I went in search of a place that would take a single woman and a large hound. I looked at apartments, rental houses, and town homes but could not find decent affordable housing.

One day I happened to be at the mailbox when the mailman arrived. The white, red, and blue jeep was being escorted down the street by a dog menagerie. Most of them were of very mixed lineage, but a few pure breeds were in the lot, including a small white poodle and an Airedale. All dogs had their tails wagging and their tongues dripping.

As the jeep slowed, I spied a box of dog biscuits on the dash.

"That's quite a menagerie you've collected," I said.

Mr. Alley looked into the center of the mass and smiled. "Yah, I collected them all along my route. Each day at the end of my run I give them all a biscuit. After they get their treat and a pat, they all go home." He smiled easily and shook his head.

"That must get pretty expensive," I replied.

"It beats getting bit."

We both chuckled at the response.

"You must be the new professor in town," he said.

"I guess so," I replied hesitantly. "The Turners have been nice enough to give me a spot on their couch and all, but I need a place to stay. My dog is proving to be a complication. But she's really good and housebroken."

"There's a house just around the corner that's going up for sale," he said. "It's a really nice house. The owner was a schoolteacher, and when she got married she rented it for a while. Now they've decided to sell. Mr. Welch is there now. You should go and take a look. It's just around the corner. 110 Alston."

He handed me the Turners' mail.

"Thanks. I'll do that."

The dogs herded the jeep up the road.

I took the mail and went into the house to cool off.

I kept thinking about what Mr. Alley had said. "Oh, it's worth a shot," I said to the dog. "Come on, Coco. Let's go for a walk." Coco and I walked up to take a look. Mr. Welch was in the front yard cleaning out the gutters.

Yes, the owner was getting ready to put the house on the market. Yes, it would be fine if I wished to see inside.

As I walked into the living room, I knew I was home.

Within a week we had closed, and my furniture was delivered.

The brick house was not air-conditioned, but it had a great attic fan. A few tips from the locals and I had mastered the art of shutting the doors, windows, and blinds during the day, and opening the house up at night. The fan provided a breeze and evaporative relief.

Each night the lows were higher, and the residual heat more oppressive.

Early one morning I heard a pop and the attic fan quit. My one coping mechanism was lost.

Grabbing the phone book, I turned to the yellow pages and quickly found the listing for electricians. I called the first name on the list. "Anthony's Electric, 25 years of experience, no job is too small." The ad was small but to the point.

Mr. Anthony answered the phone.

I explained my problem.

"Sounds like the fan belt," he said. "It won't take long to fix, but it will be two to three days before I can get there."

"Oh, no," I gasped. "I've just moved here from Wisconsin. I don't think I can stand a South Carolina night without that fan."

"I'll do what I can," he said. After giving him directions, I ended the conversation.

"Now what?" I said to Coco.

She looked confidently up at me and wagged her tail.

I found the answer at the bottom of my coffee cup. I decided to see if Mr. Anthony was correct.

The only access to the attic was through a trap door in the ceiling of the linen closet.

It was already after ten, and the outside temperature was already in the high 80's. It would be stifling hot up there. As I unloaded the few towels on the top shelf, I decided to go up in the buff. I left my hiking boots on to give me leverage and to keep the insulation from between my toes.

As soon as I poked my head through the hole, I began to sweat. I held the flashlight in my mouth as I shimmied through the hole. The fan was shrouded in dust. Mr. Anthony was right. I picked up the now linear piece of rubber that used to be the fan belt and quickly descended into the hall, closing the trap door behind me with a bang. The fan belt had broken only in one place. The neighborhood hardware store might just have a replacement.

After putting on my shirt and shorts, I walked to the store and purchased the new belt. I was back in the hall by eleven.

It was going to be an oven in the attic, but I had to get this job done.

Soon I was once again clad in only my hiking boots.

The climb perfected, I was back in the attic quicker than a breeze.

Just as I removed the paper sleeve from the belt, the doorbell rang.

"What the hay?" I muttered. "Who could that be?"

The hall was long, and the open kitchen door was in direct line with the linen closet. I could not climb out of the trap door without being in full view.

I crawled to the vent in the eaves and looked down. There in the driveway was a battered old white truck with "Anthony's Electric" painted on the door. I sat perched above the eave vent. I needed the electrician, but I did not know how to answer the door without completely exposing myself.

The back doorbell rang again.

"Sh--," I muttered but did not move.

The bell rang one more time. I watched as a man in overalls with graying hair slowly returned to his truck. A little gun of the motor and a spin of wheels on gravel and Anthony was gone.

Now I had to do the job myself or risk boiling to death in my own sweat. I was a combination of hot, mad, and disgusted. Drops of perspiration quickly covered the metal motor housing, wicking toward each other through the heavy layer of dust.

I placed the belt in the groove and gave a tug that was powered by all the adrenalin my glands had to offer.

It snapped into place.

For a moment I just sat and limply looked at it. "How did I do that?" I'm sure that was not the correct method. I looked from above and bent down and peered at it from below. It appeared to be in the correct alignment.

The slip-slide to the top shelf was easy. A skid down the wall and I was in the hall. A gentle breeze wafted in from the back door. The hall was surprisingly cool.

My hand paused for several minutes over the fan switch before I got the nerve to turn it on. The fan hummed into life. It sounded unbelievably normal.

I looked at my feet. I was surrounded by drops of water. Sweat was dripping from all points of my body.

Over the years I have needed an electrician from time to time. Each time I open the yellow pages I see the ad for Anthony's Electric. But I never call.

Wicked Wilma

AN EXTRA FIVE MINUTES can produce a life-altering event. As I drove down Plainview Drive one day, I noticed a road I had never traveled. Blessed with an extra five minutes, I decided to have a look.

As the road wound around a surprisingly beautiful spring-fed lake, I noticed a large, stately two-trunked White Oak. A stone wall had been built around it, and ivy snaked gracefully at its base. Perched squarely in front of the oak was a slightly askew and faded "for sale" sign.

I thought to myself, "No oak that magnificent should be for sale."

A cracked macadam drive serviced the far end of the property. There had obviously been a house there at one time, but it had burned.

The north edge of the property past the drive descended steeply to a rock-jumbled creek. The outlet from the lake cascaded over a series of rock shelves forming a thirty-foot waterfall.

As I descended the slope, my interest increased. This was just the habitat for Dwarf-flower Heartleaf, an endangered species I had been studying for years.

It did not take me long to find the first plant and then 1000+ more. This was the largest population I had seen in any one spot in my lifetime.

I rushed to the car, took down the realtor's name and phone number, and headed home. Barely controlling my emotions, I placed a quick call to inquire about the property. The agent told me the property had been on the market for three years. She also informed me of a "tremendous erosion problem on the back side of the property."

"That was where the plants were!" I said to myself. Verbally I said, "Yes, I know, but I think I can handle that."

She quoted me the four-acre price.

I gulped, waited, and offered her about one third of that amount.

Not believing anything would come of the query, I almost forgot about the proposal. It was a combination of confusion, excitement, and bewilderment that overwhelmed me when the realtor called several days later to tell me my offer had been accepted.

Over the next months, I designed a house to fit in the hole that was left by the former foundation. I used the same driveway, front walk, septic tank, and water line. Another bonus was the basement. It would have cost more to fill the hole than to have a whole subterranean floor.

As I began to build, the neighbors stopped by; bit by bit the story of the former owners came to light. It seems that both mother and daughter were manic-depressives. So long as the father was alive, he could keep them somewhat in balance, but with the father's death, the women were alone. Their mood swings began to synchronize and became more intense.

Wilma, the daughter, was also a drug dealer. The neighbors had stories of break-ins and thefts by Wilma or her mother. Neighbors would come home to find them wandering through their homes.

Then there was the story of the famous pizza delivery. Wilma ordered a pizza, but when it came, she hijacked the pizza deliveryman and held him hostage for twelve hours in a closet. Even today when I order pizza, two deliverymen show up.

As I wandered over the north-facing slope which housed my Dwarf-flower Heartleaf plants, I noticed that the whole hillside was pockmarked. It was as if someone had

been placer mining for gold. I asked the neighbors about the holes. No, it was not a gold mining operation. Wilma had stored her goods in mason jars and buried them on the steep slope.

Neighbors reported that after the fire, they would see flashlights shining in the woods at night as clients returned for free samples.

"What caused the fire?" I asked one day.

The neighbor reluctantly told me the story. In one of her depressions, Wilma nailed the windows of the house shut and set fire to the structure. The neighborhood watched as the house, Wilma, and her mother burned. The volunteer firemen came but without the pumper needed to retrieve water from the lake and without enough hose. By the time all equipment was on the scene, Wilma and her mother were gone.

The whole subdivision was very unsure about two more women moving into 430 Saranac Drive. Our every move was carefully scrutinized. In order to relieve the tension and anxiety, I consulted the neighbors on the color of the siding. I was leaning towards blue-gray with red shutters.

The daily walkers by said, "No, no, something bright."

The house is yellow with a warm tan roof.

Many people ask if we have ghosts.

I always reply, "If Wilma is here, she is very happy. She has filed no complaints."

The Mud Dauber and the Puritan Ethic

ONE OF THE JOYS of owning a cabin in the woods is the freedom to sit on the front porch and do absolutely nothing. To a person with an over-endowed supply of the Puritan work ethic, such an outlet is sorely needed. No one passes; no phone rings; no TV flickers, duping the individual into thinking something is being accomplished. Not a soul will know that on a given day, six hours were spent sitting on a log bench and accomplishing absolutely 0.0.

I was attempting to do exactly that one hot July afternoon when a buzz-saw-like sound caught my ear. It seemed to be coming from the bowels of the porch beam.

If one is to succeed in such a sedentary endeavor, I suggest doing it in a rented cabin. Then the sound of a buzz saw will not be so alarming, and the afternoon of emptiness will be kept intact. However, should one own the cabin, immediate visions of entropy and costly repairs are set in motion. What was that sound? Where did it come from? How costly would be the damage?

My eyes came to rest on a solitary Organ Pipe Mud Dauber busily working on a pipe of mud. Could that small insect be making all that noise? The sound occurred only when the wasp was depositing an additional layer of mud.

Well, that did it for the rest of the afternoon. I was hooked on watching this industrious wasp. If I had been content just to watch, that in itself would not have been so bad. But no, the Puritan ethic in me would not allow that. I had to get a stopwatch and time the poor thing.

Let's see, twenty-two seconds to deposit a layer of mud, 2.06 minutes to replenish the mud supply. Four and a half hours later, I had sheets of timings, and the mud dauber had a new pipe.

The making of the nest was done with a precision that would have impressed a drill sergeant. The glob of mud was carried in the chin region with the first two pairs of legs used to secure the bolus. The single wasp returned to the nest using a precise flight path, homing in on a large knot in the adjacent beam, turning in a tight parabolic path, and landing at the base of the growing pipe of drying mud. Upon landing, she would walk to the entrance. Turning around to face outward and upside down, the wasp would begin at the bottom of the pipe and lay down a bead of mud stretching from the bottom along one side of the pipe to the beam. The deposition was the part of the process that was so noisy. Perhaps it was the rapid movement of the front legs or the mouthparts, or perhaps she was just happy with her work.

Upon completion of the deposit, she would head out for yet another glob of mud. Her exit flight was as precise as her incoming one, but no parabola was swung. Two minutes later she would return with another bolus of mud, and the procedure was repeated. The parabola was swung, the landing accomplished. The crawl into the pipe was made. The only difference was that this time she would deposit the mud on the opposite side of the pipe. Thus the mud was being laid down in a herringbone pattern. Always the deposit was begun at the point furthest from the beam, but each deposit was on the opposite side of the last. At one point she took a thirty-six-minute break. When she returned, however, her next deposit was on the opposite side of the last.

Where was the male during all this industrious building? He was there, flying about, crawling in and out, inspecting her work, and trying periodically to mate with her. He appeared to be drawn to the upturned abdomen of the female exposed during the crawl into the pipe. If he was in the entrance of the pipe when the female returned, she would not land but swing another parabola and approach again. This was repeated until he decided to move. Housework was the female's duty.

After about four and a half hours of timing, I began to become curious as to what the inside of the tube looked like. Spying a newly completed pipe, I ran for the broom. A quick jab with the handle and the pipe was in pieces. In my enthusiasm for my next discovery, I had failed to close the front door, and pieces of mud pipe were everywhere.

But that was not all that was strewn all over the porch and front hall; there were bundles of spiders — live spiders. Not very lively, but a wiggle here and there proved that they were far from dead. The spiders were of various species but of fairly uniform size. Each had an abdominal diameter of 0.8 to 1.0 centimeters.

Wasp larvae were everywhere as well. The inside of the organ pipe had been chambered. Each chamber was packed with a single larva and four to six stunned spiders. The wasp apparently stung them, immobilized them, and placed them within the chamber to provide fresh meat for the growing young.

At this point in time, with my porch and front hall covered with dry bits of mud, stunned spiders and larvae, I became aware of a car coming up the long gravel drive.

How was I going to explain all of this! Surely no one would believe that anyone would voluntarily place herself ankle deep in stunned spiders.

Quickly, I began to use the business end of the broom. Too late — the car was here. My next-door neighbor had come up to tell me some news. To my surprise he was as fascinated as I was about the daubers. It could be that he was just humoring me. Come to think of it, I've not seen him since.

I never got around to cleaning up the wasp waste. Upon descending from the sleeping loft the next morning, I suddenly remembered the mess. The mud was still there, but not a spider nor larva was to be found. A quick check of my microscope showed a lone, stunned spider still where I had been looking at it the previous day. The larvae and the spiders hadn't walked off.

Did the wasp return to claim her own? Did another animal, such as the many skinks that inhabit the mountain with me, have a free lunch?

Well, there goes another afternoon. Such questions are far too important not to explore — especially being over endowed with the Puritan work ethic.

Notes on the natural history of the organ pipe mud dauber:

The organ pipe mud dauber (*Trypoxylon albitarsis*) is a quite common solitary wasp belonging to the family Sphecidae. This species is shiny and black except for the white tarsi (the outermost segment of each leg). The white tarsus is the characteristic used to derive its species name.

The mud tubes are often placed in groups of two or three on exposed beams of barns and porches. Each tube contains a number of chambers. Each chamber contains a single larva and several stunned spiders to be used as larval food. When the larva matures into an adult and is ready to emerge, it makes a hole through the exposed side of the earthen tube.

Information from S.W. Frost, 1959. *Insect Life and Insect Natural History*. Dover Press, p. 266.

Aqueous Humor

TODAY WAS A DAY in which I could not keep water in my car or out of my house.

Oh, the day began peacefully enough, with an unusually red rosy sunrise. The ease at which the orb slipped over the horizon and over the nude fall ridges gave no hint of the day's problems to come.

The early hours were filled with success. After downing two steaming cups of coffee while watching the sun's progress and ultimate success, I felled two small trees. The ax was dull and the chainsaw was out of oil, so I gnawed them down with a handsaw meant for ripping sheets of paper-thin plywood.

While cutting, I mused that the easy way is usually not the way things are done here at the cabin. In the early morning, I actually thought that was an advantage.

The two-inch diameter trees only took fifteen minutes to fell, and I was pleased. The next job was to fix the gravel step which had begun to show advanced stages of entropy. Success was achieved here, too.

With these two accomplishments under my belt, I tackled the plumbing. The night before, I had noticed a green telltale trickle creeping out from under the faucet in the washroom. A little bolt tightening was all that was required. Surely I could handle that. Besides, I had bought a crescent wrench the week before and could not wait to try it out.

A quick turn and a mini-geyser hit me squarely in the left breast pocket. A quick turn of the nut in the opposite direction rapidly increased the flow, directing it at my right breast pocket.

I backed the bolt off and succeeded in moderating the flow. Now the water no longer cascaded off my body but slowly ran down the inside of the wall. Dumbfounded, I stood listening to the dripping water from the studs and envisioned the invasion of a new virulent strain of slime mold — one of those house-consuming slimes that only grows on mountain cabins owned by do-it-yourself mechanical morons.

I had an idea: "Turn off the water pump." That would stop the flood. In my normal cool manner, I ran to the fuse box and flipped the switch labeled "water pump" to off. Slowly I returned to the washroom, sure that I would find the water trickle stopped. But no, the trickle continued.

Strange. Residual pressure?

I opened the faucet. Any portion of my body that had survived the initial baptism was inundated by the deluge that came from the tap.

Very strange.

I filled every vessel in the kitchen before I realized that perhaps the fuse was mislabeled. Returning to the fuse box, I turned off the main switch. The stream slowed and finally stopped.

Several days earlier I had seen an ad for a magic compound in a spray can that stopped leaks, cured gutter rot, patched up holes in truck tires, and probably healed marriages. Surely that would work. Town was only ten minutes away, and there was one hardware store open on Saturday. Off I went. Convinced I would be back shortly, I did not bother to lock the cabin.

As I descended from my mountain retreat, the truck sounded strange, sort of like a colony of crickets had taken up residence under the hood. The power was fine, and Beethoven's Sixth was playing on the classical radio station. The pastoral landscape matched well with the music, and the crickets seemed to chirp in tune. The gauges all were normal, but just in case, I decided to stop at the only gas station with an attendant and have him listen to my crickets.

The grease-smeared attendant diagnosed the problem with impressive ease. "Ma'am, it's your water pump. See, it's not supposed to move like this." He grabbed it and wiggled it in more directions than are found on a cheap compass.

"Can I drive it?" I asked.

"For a block or two, maybe 25 or 30 miles, but not to Pittsburgh."

"Can you fix it?"

"No, but they might have one in town."

I thanked him and filled the tank. That's optimism for you. The truck may not get two blocks, but I was getting a full tank.

Bumfuzzled, I continued to the hardware store, fully realizing that I could not make it back to the cabin.

As I walked in concentric circles in the store that had been reshuffled and turned upside-sidewise since my last visit, I ran into Kyle, a former student.

"How are things?" he innocently asked.

"Well," and I told him my water problems.

"No problem, there's a junk auto parts store in the next block. They will have a pump. You get the pump and I'll put it in. Then I'll ride up to your cabin this afternoon and fix the faucet. It probably just needs a washer."

I scooted around to the junkyard and inquired about a pump.

"Do you have a water pump for a D-50 pickup, 1980 model?"

The store clerk disappeared and returned with a pump. "I only have the 1979, but I think it will fit."

I returned to the hardware store with the pump just as Kyle was finishing his purchases.

He grabbed a tool kit from the front of his truck and began the operation. He was a magician. With the ease of buttering bread, he removed the wiggle-wrought water pump and slipped the new one in place. It fit perfectly.

All the while I was trying to remember how Kyle had done in my class. I knew he was not an outstanding student; I just hoped and prayed that I hadn't flunked him.

"If it's good for you, I can follow you back to your cabin and have a look at that faucet."

"How wonderful! Thanks."

Kyle was as good as his word.

The secret to plumbing is having a wrench in both hands and a spare rubber washer. With that skill, a fitting can be tightened without filling either breast pocket or washing one stud.

Now I have a new problem. Should I buy a second wrench or a bow saw?

I Was Not Meant to Be a Mother

THERE ARE MANY THINGS I don't do well. I can't cook. I clean only when I have lost something. I play tennis like a moose, and I'm a terrible mother.

This last revelation came to me last summer. I was sitting on the front porch of the log cabin attempting to plan a new course which I was to teach at the university. The effort was doomed for failure. The course was three months away. The temperature was hovering in the high 80's, and the moon was not in the right quarter for such deep thoughts. As I sat there intent on being diligent, I kept hearing peeping sounds coming from under the porch. Finally, it dawned on me that this was not just any peeping but was a frantic, advanced, terrified peeping. It was constant and ever increasing in intensity.

As I crawled under the porch, I was not sure what I would find, and I was even less sure of what I could do about the problem.

As my eyes got accustomed to the light, I located a nest up under the support posts, nestled between the cross-beams. Poking out of the very skewed nest were three gaping red mouths. The loudest peeping was not coming from the nest, however. There on the ground beneath the nest lay one very distraught baby bird. What kind it was I could not tell. It had a small egg-shaped bottom and a translucent breast through which I could see the fluttering heart. Its eyes were closed, and it had a mouth as big as my thumb.

I bent down to pick it up. But before I touched it, I

thought better of it. What if the mother smelled people on the peeper? She might reject it.

I sat back on my haunches wondering what to do. How long I sat there I cannot tell you.

But as I looked around, I spied a flattened stick and an old paint stirrer. If I could pick the bird up using these sticks like chopsticks, I could get the job done without touching it.

As I approached the bird with a stick in each hand, the peeping increased. After several false attempts, I managed to prop the bird up on the paint stirrer and slowly lift it to the nest. It teetered precariously on the stick but did not fall.

Approaching the nest, I realized there was yet another challenge to be faced. The stirrer was too big to allow the bird to be placed in the nest. I knew not to touch the bird with my hands.

The only solution appeared to be to flip the bird into the nest. Using my best pancake flipping technique, I let the bird go.

It made one beautifully symmetrical loop in the air and landed in the center of the nest. One slight problem remained. The bird landed on its head.

Taking smaller sticks, I gradually righted the little thing. All four were safely in the nest, beak side up.

As I crawled out from under the porch, I was sure I had saved one doomed bird.

Over the course of the afternoon I got quite good at bird tossing. No fewer than four times I had to crawl under the porch and retest my skills. By late afternoon all four birds were on the ground, and there was no sign of mother.

It finally dawned on me that this tossing might not be the best thing for growing birds. The squalid nest was at the wrong angle for the retention of heaved chicks. The nest was falling apart. I tried to build a nest on the ground. I arranged sticks in the shape of a nest and lined it with toilet paper. Using the paint stirrer, I maneuvered the birds into the new nest.

Maybe my presence on the porch was preventing the return of the mother. It was getting late anyway, and all that crawling under the porch had made me hungry.

As I prepared my meal of hot dogs and boiled green beans, I wondered if the birds might need some food. Green beans would surely not work, but how about little bites of hot dog?

Birds do not like hot dogs. No matter how you dice or slice them, birds will not touch them.

As I sat in the living room wondering what to do next, I again heard loud peeping sounds. I wandered about the room trying to locate the sound. It was loudest near the fireplace. I crawled into the ashes. It was definitely loudest here. Opening the damper caused a shower of soot to fall, covering my face and upper body. Never open the damper with your mouth open.

I was sitting in the fireplace spitting soot out of my mouth when I noticed the silhouette of a mother bird dangling upside down in the chimney feeding three or four hungry beaks.

Was she feeding them insects?

Out of the fireplace I came and hurried to the windowsill. I knew there were plenty of dead insects there. With tweezers I plucked up the most luscious morsels and headed for the porch.

After gagging several birds, I decided these must be too large and returned to the house to harvest the smaller insects. Flies were too big as well. Toenail clippers reduced their size, but the birds could not handle even half a fly. No matter how hard I tried or how small the pieces, the birds would not take my offerings.

As I slowly entered the house, I spied a fly buzzing from one windowpane to the other.

Maybe they liked only fresh meat!

But hitting a fly on a warm evening when you don't have a fly swatter is no easy feat.

I tried numerous implements — shoes, belts, books —

but settled on a pancake turner. It was a slow business.

The speed was all-important. Too fast and all you got was a black smear. Too slow and no fly. It took fifteen minutes, but I finally had a small pile of stunned flies.

The results were the same. The baby birds only choked on the fresh offerings.

It wasn't thirty minutes later that a commotion from the chimney again took me away from my work. The mother had returned with a fresh supply of food.

I crawled back into the fireplace to get another lesson on mother birding. Closely I followed her antics. There she was standing upside down in the chimney, her mouth wide open, and baby birds were reaching way down into her throat. She was feeding them regurgitated bugs.

There is a limit to my desire to be a mother. I was not ready to go that far for four birds.

I would compromise. There were still a few flies left. I made a mixture of flies and human saliva.

By this time the light was fading fast, and I could hardly make out the open mouths in my makeshift nest. The peeping was much fainter now, and the mouths were not all open. By tapping the tip of the beak, I could get the birds to open their mouths, but they rapidly closed them again when they discovered my offering. No matter what proportion of fly to saliva, they were not interested.

I gave up. Maybe the mother bird would return by morning, but by then, it would probably be too late.

The day of crawling in and out from under the porch had worn me out. I went to bed early and slept well.

Early the next morning the dog woke me. She was barking wildly downstairs. Sleep was impossible.

As I trundled down the steps, I saw her barking with her head in the corner of the living room.

As I approached, I quickly saw the problem. The night before, I had failed to close the damper. There in the corner was one of the well-fed members of the chimney flock. It was trying desperately to fly up the corner of the room.

I grabbed it about 1.5 feet off the floor and headed for the fireplace.

I laid it gently in the ashes and closed the doors. The nest was not six feet above it. Maybe it could fly up to its nest.

After making a pot of coffee and drinking a couple of cups, I went to check on my porch brood. All that was left was a few shreds of toilet paper. Not a bird was in sight. The nest was still and quiet.

I suspect Heriot, the hognose snake, had a very good dinner last night.

An hour passed, and I went to check on my fledgling in the fireplace. It was still there, and it was obviously tiring. Two feet was about as high as it could get, and then it would settle back into the ashes.

I had to do something.

Gently, I placed my hands around the bird. It struggled very little. I lifted it as high as I could and opened my hands. It did not move.

Now what!

Desperation set in. I could not take another failure.

Quickly, I lowered my hands and then threw the fledgling up the chimney. Hopefully, I would get it high enough so that the bird could regain the nest.

The bird flapped like hell.

Soot covered my hands and face and filled my eyes.

I don't know where the fledgling got to, but it never came down.

I closed the damper and crawled out of the fireplace for the last time.

I have learned a lesson. No matter how loud or long the peeping, I will not answer. I now know that I was not meant to be a mother.

A Saturday in August

IT WAS A SATURDAY at the end of August. After a long hot summer, an August day with a forecast high of 90 degrees was a relief. Earlier in the week, a drought-breaking rain had fallen, refreshing the long parched earth. It was now possible to get some outside chores done.

While sipping my morning cups of coffee, I turned my attention to the heap of newspapers, magazines, and junk mail that overflowed the recycling bin under the end table.

"Well, today would be a good day to tame that pile," I thought. The rest of the household must have concurred, for Mary, my housemate, appeared with bags, and Georgina, our student boarder, agreed to help with the project.

Within minutes the car was filled with boxes, bags, and plastic sacks containing a summer's accumulation of waste paper.

On the short drive to the recycling center, we passed a team of volunteer firemen with boots extended asking for donations. I skillfully avoided their outstretched boots by rounding the corner as the light turned amber.

As we began to sort out the debris pile, a cool breeze rustled the leaves on weed trees behind the dumpsters. The recycling center is at the side of a long abandoned grocery store. The space is cramped. To allow cars to turn around, the motley array of dumpsters is placed end to end at the very edge of the tarmac. No two bins are exactly alike. Some are rusted red, others are green, and still others are rusty dusty blue. The can bins are cages teetering on a single axle, while the paper, plastic, and glass bins are variations on the theme of a standard forklift-emptied dumpster. Sun faded plastic decals inform the recycler of the appropriate container for mixed paper, #1 plastic, #2 plastic, tin cans, aluminum cans, and various colors of glass.

As most of our goods came under the category of "mixed paper," I parked nearest the two red and one dirty blue containers for paper. The next dumpster in line was a blue container similar to the blue mixed paper. Its label read "#2 Plastic Only."

Quickly, we began trudging up and down the line of steel boxes trying to decipher the cryptic messages on the fading signs.

Finally, only one bag of mixed paper remained. I grabbed it with gusto and aimed it at one of the blue dumpsters. The arc was perfect. The paper bag sailed over the side and disappeared into the bowels of the steel monster.

It was only after I heard the thud that I realized that I had aimed at the wrong blue box.

I crawled up onto the flat metal plate at the top of the forklift housing. Standing on my tiptoes, I could barely see over the side. The bin was almost empty. The bottom was covered with an array of motley colored plastic bottles. One lone paper sack filled with newspaper lay on its side at the far end of the dumpster.

"Now what?" Georgina asked.

"Well, we can't leave it there."

After an endless moment, Georgina suggested, "Maybe that gas station over there has a ladder we could use to get inside."

"Probably not," I said. "Besides, getting in is not the problem. It's getting out."

The tarmac was heating up rapidly.

"Oh, well, we know there is a fire station down the road. If I get stuck, you can get a ladder from them."

I climbed up onto the forklift housing. The rim was reached surprisingly easily. The controlled fall into the dumpster went quite well. Until I got to the bottom.

The thunderstorm of a few days before had filled the open-topped dumpster with three inches of very stagnant water. The water lapped over my sandals and wicked up my dark blue socks.

The bag of newspaper had escaped the dousing. It was floating above the water on a raft of half sunken plastic milk jugs.

I splashed over to it and quickly threw it over the side to Georgina.

From the inside, the rusty walls of the dumpster looked much higher. About midway up the side was a small ridge. If I could somehow support myself on that ridge, I could get a purchase on the top rim and shimmy over the wall. But I couldn't get my foot up to the ridge.

Suddenly, a yellow bucket was dangling over my head.

"Here, try this," Georgina said.

Sure enough, the bucket provided just the height required to make it to the ridge. A quick pull-up and I was teetering on top of the dumpster. One jump-step to the fork-lift housing and I was out.

"You forgot the bucket."

"How could I get the bucket? I was standing on it," I lamented. "Well, how are we going to get it out? It's a number 6 bucket in a #2 plastic world."

"How about those metal survey flags in your trunk?" Georgina asked.

We made a hook at one end of a yellow flagged wire and lengthened the hook by attaching a white flagged wire to the other end. The joint between the flags made our magic wand very wiggly.

I climbed back up onto the rim of the dumpster and slowly lowered our hooked wand.

There were two holes in the bottom of the bucket. But every time I even touched the bucket, the wand would bend at the joint. Finally I spied the bucket handle perfectly propped on a floating yellow jug. I eased the hook around the handle and slowly pulled. The handle slipped easily into the hook. A gentle pull and the bucket was back on dry land.

As I climbed down, I noticed an elderly man wearing a straw hat and light pants leaning on the driver's door of an old car. He had parked in the shade and apparently had watched the whole extraction procedure.

"I got my mixed paper all mixed up," I said lamely.

"I commend you for your efforts and your agility. Most people would have just left the mess."

"Well, let's put it this way," I said. "I'm more agile than I thought."

On the way home the firemen were still at the corner and the light was green. I slowed, rolled down my window, and tossed $5.00 into the extended boot. You can never buy too much insurance.

Several days later as I was turning into my driveway, I noticed a large bright red tag hanging from my front door. It was impossible to know how long it had been there, as only strangers use the front door.

I stopped the car and made it slowly up the walk. It had been a long day. I slowly took the tag off the doorknob and read: YOU HAVE BEEN FOUND TO BE LITTERING AT THE FERNWOOD GLENDALE RECYCLING CENTER. IF YOU DO NOT CALL THE NUMBER BELOW WITHIN 48 HOURS, YOU WILL BE FINED $1,000.00.

How long had this notice been hanging on the front door? I might already owe $1,000.00. I was mad, confused, and disgusted. There is not an English word to describe the seething rage coursing through my body. It was after 5:00. I would get no answers until Monday.

Early on Monday, just as the environmental police were sitting down to their desks, I was in their ear demanding an explanation.

"Well, ma'am, a piece of litter with your name on it was found in the plastic bin when it was dumped the other day. This is a violation that supports a fine of $1,000.00."

"How could this be? I am always very careful at the recycling center and even pick up the litter of others," I pleaded. Then I remembered the last trip to the dumpster. So I told him the tale you already know.

"Well, ma'am," he said. "I'll have to believe you, a story like that just can't be made up." He chided me on entering the dumpster. "That's very dangerous. One of our men got stabbed by an old hypodermic needle just yesterday pulling stuff out of one of the dumpsters. If you put something in the wrong dumpster in the future, just call and tell us."

That was that. I was exonerated. But I still wasn't satisfied. I had been on the initial committee that started the recycling program in our town. I despised the tone of the missile and realized if I was having trouble making out the signage on the faded dumpsters, others were having the same trouble.

I happened to know the current head of the recycling program and gave her a call. I told her of my plight, my fine, and my abhorrence at the tone of the letter. I also suggested that if I was having problems making out the signs, then others must have been making the same mistake.

She listened quietly, even laughed at my plight. "Painting and new signage are expensive," she cautioned. "Our budget is tight, very tight." Then there was that long do-nothing pause followed by an apologetic, "We do have some new signs on the way." She thanked me for bringing this to her attention, and we amicably ended our conversation.

The whole incident was slowly fading into distant memory when I again made my pilgrimage to the recycling center. The whole line of dumpsters had received a color coordinated face lift, complete with bright color coordinated signs. I just stopped and stared. What happened? Only weeks before, I had been told this was impossible.

Maybe my tour of the inside of the dumpster was not in vain. Or maybe there were other dumpster divers who had a similar tale to tell. I would like to think I had something to do with it, but it most likely was my old friend serendipity.

My New Housemate

THE OTHER EVENING my two ditch dogs (strays found at the edge of roads) began a frenzied chorus of barking from the small library adjacent to the living room. Similar choruses could indicate the presence of a passing golf cart used by my neighbor to walk his dog. But this cacophony seemed more intense than usual.

As I entered the small light-flooded library, the two dogs were dancing around an anaconda-sized black snake coiled in the middle of the rug. It was striking outwards at the legs of the vertically bouncing pups.

THE SNAKE was at least four feet long but very skinny. Who knows how long it had been my housemate? Its last meal had been a very long time ago.

I grabbed the dogs, threw them into the living room, and shut the door. As I patted the closed door, I realized that the crack beneath it was less then snake proof. A rug weighed down by Civil War history books clogged the crevasse. It's a good thing that the Civil War was a long one.

I grabbed a broom, took several deep breaths, opened the door a crack and peeped in. The snake was mimicking a large cow pie perched squarely in the center of the rug. I quickly closed the door.

From the sunroom I could reach the library's sliding door that opened onto the deck. The cow pie was still there.

The door opened easily, allowing the snake a graceful exit path.

Then my broom and I sat in the sunroom waiting for the snake to take the honorable path and slither onto the deck.

The snake, however, chose to unfold and slowly make its way into a bookcase, where it propped its head on *The Rise and Fall of the Third Reich*.

I waited.

No movement except for my hands which were shaking so much I could have used them to churn butter with the broom.

Forty-five minutes passed.

It began to drizzle.

Was the head emerging, or was it just my imagination?

Yes — Ever so slowly a slithering began. This snake was so slow it would have lost a race with a three-legged ant. Time seemed limitless.

Eventually, the snake made its way along the floorboards and propped its head on the doorsill. Indecision was its only instinct.

Another three quarters of an hour elapsed before its tail crossed the threshold, allowing the whole snake to emerge onto the deck.

The passage along the deck was so slow that one needed a time-lapse camera to note progress.

Snakes are not designed to go down steps, and there were fourteen steps to the safety of the ivy patch below. For a long time the snake straddled the top step, narrowly missing a small hole in the siding that could have been the original entrance pore.

All motion stopped.

The rain continued.

It was only when the snake got to the banister that the slither speed increased, and exit was assured.

After toweling down, I replaced the broom and unleashed the hounds.

Both dogs ran to the spot of their snake encounter and began rolling on the rug. I could smell nothing, but to them snake musk was a wondrous find, thus confirming that what is a stink to some is perfume to others.

The Taurus and the Bull

IT WAS AUGUST, mating season for bison in Yellowstone National Park. I had rented a Taurus at the Jackson Hole Airport and headed north for four days of exploration and nature photography.

The sagebrush-dotted flatlands were surprisingly green after a summer of above normal rainfall. The gray-green of the sage stood out in sharp contrast to the green grass. Splashes of color produced by fields of Purple Lupine, Scarlet Gilia, and the school bus yellow flowers of Mule's Ears punctuated the valley of the Snake River. As I drove north, the Tetons were on my left, rising like a saw blade perched upright at the edge of a flower-strewn tablecloth.

There was a chill in the air. Winter was hiding behind those mountain peaks and would soon drain southward through the passes.

The wildlife was almost as abundant as the tourists as I drove into the park heading for Yellowstone Lodge. The westward ride into morning had made for a very long day. As I approached the lodge, I drove through a large herd of buffalo. Here is where I would come tomorrow for photographs.

Up early the next morning, I emerged after the bison and before the tourists.

The early morning light cast long shadows on the sage. Paired bison were distributed in surprising uniformity across the open expanses.

I parked near an amorous pair and took aim through the passenger window with my Nikon.

The bull was on the far side of the cow. She was nestled close to his side with her head at his shoulders. A tuft of grass was hanging from his mouth, and a deep guttural rumble rose from his throat. Two biological urges were in major combat: the need to add bulk for the long, hard winter and the urge for genetic immortality.

The variations in vocal utterances while still chewing grass were astonishing. I expected him to choke at any moment.

The pair moved as one. All the bison couples were performing the same slow dance.

I had my eye frozen to the viewfinder. My arms were askew to form a human tripod. The prize-winning photo of the amorous couple was squarely in my viewfinder, and my finger was poised to freeze this couple in time.

Suddenly the car lurched violently to the right. I turned in time to see two very large nostrils pressed firmly on the driver's side window surrounded by two huge circles of condensation. A large male bison was trying to move the car out of his way.

In my haste to get the perfect shot, I had not noticed

a lone bull wading slowly across the Yellowstone River. The Taurus was directly between the new suitor and his intended conquest. He was clearing the way for the ensuing battle.

The keys were in the ignition, and the engine quickly returned to life. I yanked the car into gear. The car swerved first to the left and then back to the right before regaining the pavement. Only the massive front portion of the bison festooned with matted hair was visible in the rear view mirror as I negotiated these maneuvers.

Returning to the lodge, I surveyed the damage to the rental car. If you placed your eye over the driver-side headlight and sighted toward the rear, a telltale bison dent could easily be seen. It was only semi-visible if you looked at the vehicle from the side.

As I was assessing the damage, the lodge handyman came up. "You got a problem?" he asked.

"Yeah," I replied. "I got between two bull bison fighting over a cow."

He looked at the damage for a moment. "Got a toilet plunger?" he asked.

"No," I said. "I sort of left home without it."

"Well," he said, "I might be able to find one."

He was gone, leaving me in the driveway with the bison-dented body.

I busied myself reorganizing my mess. I was not sure whether he would return, but I didn't want to leave, either. About five minutes passed before the mountain of a mechanic returned with a plunger in hand.

He wet the plunger and placed it in the center of the dent and pulled. The dent disappeared like a popped blister.

I was amazed. "Thank you," was all I could manage at first. But then I added, "You must have done that before. Do you get a lot of bison dents around here?"

"No," he said, "but it's mating season and bison tend to get their way this time of year."

When I returned the Taurus to the rental office, I never

mentioned the bison bashing. It was hard to notice the dent unless you had your eye aimed at just the right angle. The patina of dust also added a bit of camouflage.

"Besides," I rationalized, "if they name a car Taurus, they should expect something like this to happen — at least in Yellowstone during the mating season."

A Thanksgiving for Three

OUR FAMILY was very small, just Mom, Dad, and me. After the death of my grandparents, there was not the critical mass needed for holiday celebrations. Too much work was divided among too few people.

My father was a struggling art teacher, and my mother was a homemaker. To make matters worse, my mother could not cook.

Thanksgivings came and went with an assortment of very crisp birds and underdone fowl.

One Thanksgiving my father came home with a burlap sack held out in front of him at arm's length. His head was turned to the side, forcing him to negotiate doorways without any depth perception. It was a feat done with only limited success.

"What's in the sack, Jack?" my mother said.

"One of my students gave us a turkey for Thanksgiving."

At that exact instant the sack took a sudden lunge to the left, forcing my father into the nearest wall.

"My God," my mother said. "That bird's still alive!"

"Very," my father replied.

At this point I entered the discussion. "Let me see. Let me see." Dad opened the sack and held it low so I could look.

The smell hit me first. It was an acrid, earthy, warm sort of odor. Inside was the most disheveled bird I had ever seen. The bird was matted with droppings.

"Ugh!" was all I could muster.

"How long has he been in that sack?" Mom asked.

"All day. I couldn't leave him in the studio so I put him in the trunk with a bag of ice."

"Well, what are you going to do with him now?" Mother continued.

"Kill him, I guess."

"Jack, I don't know how to kill a bird and you don't either." Mother had reached her semi-excited, semi-exasperated state.

Dad thought for a moment. "I bet Arthur does," he quietly replied.

Arthur was our next-door neighbor. So Dad, the sack, and I went to visit Arthur.

"You'll need an ax," Arthur said.

"I don't have one," my father said apologetically. "Will a big kitchen knife do?"

"Nope," was the reply. "But I think I have an old ax in the shed you can borrow," and with that, Arthur disappeared.

Dad was quiet for a time and so was the sack. He cautiously opened the top to make sure he still needed that ax.

He did.

Arthur returned with a rusty old model with half the handle missing.

"You can use that old stump in your back yard. Get Kathryn to hold the bird down, and just chop off his head." This concluded Arthur's lesson on the killing of poultry.

Mom and Dad headed for the stump. They told me to stay inside and get ready for Mandy's birthday party.

This was going to be a fun party. All the kids were going. Mandy and I were not close friends, but I was so happy she had included me.

I had just finished putting on my new white dress. Mother had spent endless hours on it. She was a superb seamstress. On this dress she had experimented with smocking techniques. It was beautiful. White socks and shiny white shoes completed the outfit.

Suddenly, there was a terrible commotion coming from

the back yard. I ran out the back door just in time to collide with a panic-stricken Tom turkey with his head dangling to one side. Blood spurted from a severed carotid artery. It made a perfect arc, landing as a red streak in the center of my front. The smocking soaked it in like a sponge.

The scene was easy to piece together. Mother had been holding Tom down on the stump. Dad had taken aim with Arthur's ax. Whether Mom moved or Dad missed, I'm not quite sure. But probably they both just shut their eyes and hoped. Anyway, Tom's neck was not completely severed. In the horror of it all, Mom lost her grip. Tom quickly sensed the opportunity and escaped.

Eventually, he bled out and collapsed at the far end of the yard, but not without decorating most of the yard with turkey blood.

The job was not finished. They had to dress the bird. This, too, was new territory. Mom went into the house to get tweezers and began plucking out feathers one by one.

Arthur had heard the noise too and came over to investigate. When he saw my mother sitting on the back steps covered in feathers and blood, plucking out each feather, he said, "My God, Woman, dunk that sucker in hot water!"

"I'm not ready to cook it," Mother replied.

"No, you're not going to boil it. You're just going to loosen the feathers so they will come out easier."

The bird was plucked, gutted, and washed and washed and washed.

When Tom arrived at the table, he was a crisp brown with a halo of burnt feathers.

The peas and mashed potatoes were passed. Tom was carved, but none of us would eat him. The family and Tom had suffered enough.

Tom was placed in a small grave in the back yard feathered with his own down.

For several years our Thanksgivings were even more perfunctory. Turkey was never part of the menu. We always had chicken.

The Unknown Keeps On Giving

IT'S CHRISTMAS time again. A time for cash and bash, a time for overconsumption and overexpectations.

As I was worrying about the perfect gift in the correct size and color, my mind wandered back to last Christmas.

For several years I have not bothered with decorations, cards, or a tree. All that effort only promotes the spending of six to seven hours on the first day of the new year cleaning up after the old before one can think about the new. Cleaning is not a pleasant occupation on any day and an abhorrence on the first day of a new year.

The spirit of the holidays for me is in the gift giving. I don't shop, but starting in September, I seem to spend my odd moments drifting aimlessly through catalogs. Each year the catalog pile grows. Now two tables, a bookshelf, and a wastebasket are lost under my catalog pile. I can select anything from a 47-blade pocketknife, a home computerized robot, or a jogging suit already decorated with muddy footprints from the neighbor's dog, cat, or rabbit, a truly thoughtful present for the jogger who insists on running in the rain.

Books by mail provide an extra bonus. You can order them in September, read them in October and November, and wrap them in December. If you're careful, the book can still look new. If not, you can say you were just interested in providing a quality controlled Christmas.

But the real joy of the catalog is the potential package perched on the woodpile by the back door at the close of every day. What a welcoming sight after another twelve-hour non-productive day to see that mysterious brown box. Which is it? What is it? Who's it for? Of course, a few things must be purchased for your own consumption to enhance this childish craving.

The nicest parcel left last year at my back door did not arrive by FedEx or from the United States Postal Service. The mystery of its delivery is still intact.

After a particularly hectic week, I found on my back stoop, draped in red bows and bright green foil, the most perfect little Norfolk Island pine tree. No note, not a word of cheer could be found among its boughs. Just the cheeriest of plants left totally incognito.

I didn't have any plants. They always died from my neglect. But not this one. Every time I look at it I get a warm feeling that starts at my sternum and radiates outwards.

Over the weeks after the tree drop, I asked all my friends if they had lost a tree at my doorstep. No one knew a thing about a wayward tree. It could have been any of them. It could have been left by mistake, meant for the little old lady next door. Perhaps the card just fell off and was lost forever in my woodpile. It doesn't matter. I appreciate the tree more for not knowing the giver. What a truly beautiful gift. A selfless gift that has brought me more joy from the mystery than ever would have been gained with the addition of a card.

This year I plan to give a few gifts without cards. I hope that they will give the recipient at least half the joy that the Yule pine has given me.

Oh, yes, I got some new red bows for the pine this year. It only seems right to play it again. Thanks, Sam?

The Sweet Scent of Home

THERE IS A FEELING I get when I turn at the base of the hill onto Dickinson Avenue that I can't get on any other street in the world. It's the sense of coming home again.

True, Clark's old brick filling station at the corner has metamorphosed into an insurance office. The hill on the left where we used to sled is now covered with the sameness of suburban sprawl. The apple trees in the orchard below the house have all died, and the stone fishpond in the lower lot no longer holds water. Housing developments have sprung up at the top of the hill, and new families have moved into the neighborhood, altering the cadence of the community.

But there are those clues that defy change. There is the scar on the old maple where my cousin, Robert Lee, crashed the car on his first solo driving lesson at the age of three. The tree and the family remember.

The hill is just as steep and the road just as uneven.

If I squint, I can still see the old Ford truck of the butcher making the turn at the tip of the hill. The bed of the truck is covered with ice. Lying in that chilling bed are fresh cuts of meat — pork chops, roasts, hams, and pails of hamburger. Under the seat he always had tins of Snyder pretzels. Gramma could trade in an old tin for a fresh, full one. The pretzels were better then, bigger, crisper, and oh, so special.

The house at 220 Dickinson looks surprisingly the same. True, it has been shielded with new vinyl siding, but it's still a glistening white with black accents. The same breeze-catching wrap-around porch is still there with its corner-hung swing.

The smells are the same, too. The old wood has captured all the odors of daily life. The smell of baked bread, frying bacon, and burnt toast — the smells of celebratory dinners, my uncle's pipe, and my grandmother's canning have been soaked up like a sponge.

The warmth of present life is infused with the odors of the past.

The long front hall that extends the full length of the house is unaltered. Ancient plants in older pots form a jungle in the bay window to the right of the front door. Scars and mars from an unending parade of young children and dogs are etched in the dark woodwork.

When I was young, Uncle Bill and Uncle Carl would build extensive model train layouts the full length of the hall. They would start in September and be making the finishing touches on the display as late as Christmas week. Artistic layout was honed to perfection when my cousin, Ruth Ann, added her skills.

If you look at just the right angle, you can make out the outline of the layouts still.

But it's not the scars and mars I come to see. It's a family that has accepted me as their own.

The warmth of affection, the interwoven lives, and the want of each other's company make this house a home.

At Christmas, every card that is received is placed on ribbons that decorate the massive wooden doors of the once formal living room. On the mantel there is a stocking for every member of the family. There is even one for me.

I'm not really a member of this family — technically. We have no genes in common. My stepmother has the genetic ties. But she will not be here for Christmas, and there is no stocking with her name on it.

Robert Frost said that home is a place where if you have to go there, they have to take you in.

But they don't have to do anything for me.

After my father died, my mother and her family drifted apart. For years there was little contact between my mother and her family. When her sister died, she did not go home. When her mother died many years later, the response was the same.

But Uncle Bill called to tell me of my grandmother's passing. I went to the funeral. Because of dementia she had not known anyone for years. The death was a relief, and the gathering was a reunion rather than a wake.

I found my way unerringly to Clark's filling station. The ruts in the road were old friends. As I walked up onto the porch, there was that smell, an odor that I had not sensed in years.

As I opened the screen door, the squeak was a familiar one.

I took a big breath, knocked, and opened the front door.

It was as if I hadn't been gone a day. We had all aged but to the same degree. Our relative positions in the family had not changed. I was home again.

I took a big whiff. Yep, it was where I belonged.

The Study

THE LATE AFTERNOON SUN streamed in through the glass panes of the study doors, casting brilliant parallelograms of light on the red Persian carpet. An ancient gray cat lay curled in the center of one of the geometric light patches. Its body was perfectly positioned, having been honed by years of basking, to absorb the optimum amount of heat from the late summer sun.

An aroma of must filled the room. It was a complex odor, generated from the mixing of scents from maturing carpet, aging prints, old paint, ancient texts, and well-seasoned wood. The walls of the study were lined with books precisely placed on the dark mahogany shelves that covered every inch of wall space. The colors in the carpet were mirrored in the spines of the books lining the shelves. A large gate-legged table dominated the center of the room. It had once occupied a crevice in a French chalet, but for many years now, it had stood in the very center of the study. Disheveled piles of yellowing maps and archaeological drawings were piled on its expansive surface. Rolled maps poked out at odd angles from the odd-shaped spaces between its legs.

A large stone fireplace interrupted the expanse of shelves on the northern wall. Gas burning logs had been implanted in the firebox. Though cleaner and more easily cared for, they provided only a visual image of warmth on a winter's eve.

The study was a room that was both restful and yet

nurtured the thought process. It was a sanctuary of silence where thoughts could be played out into symphonies of ideas, then discarded after hours of careful perusal. Here favorite theories could be reevaluated and new ones formulated without the fear of interruption.

Whenever Jack entered the room, he always stood for a moment at the door and took in a deep breath. He could feel himself relax. Just rubbing the dark wood of the doorframe connected him with the history of the place. He could still see his anthropologist father, whom he was trying to emulate, busily at work on his manuscripts. All six of his father's books had been written in longhand at the roll-top desk still precisely centered between the glass paned doors opening into the rose garden.

The cat felt it, too. Both Jack and the cat fit into the complex patterns played out throughout the room. Although the cat never stirred, Jack knew that his presence had been noted.

It was his routine to fold himself into the recliner near the stone fireplace and read the paper. The cat would substitute Jack's lap for her solar heated carpet only after the sun slipped behind the poplars at the edge of the garden.

As darkness filled in the patches, Jack absentmindedly petted the cat while carefully reading in between the lines of the *New York Times*. A barely audible purr was the only sound. It and the quiet room helped to bring Jack's blood pressure and his sense of what was important into tolerable limits.

It was only after the corners of the room were completely shrouded in darkness that Jack moved over to the desk, turned on the green global light centered over the work surface, and began piecing together fractured remains from the past.

The reawakening of intellectual curiosity was not the result of the room or the cat, but a synergism between the physical and animal worlds that neither alone could have achieved.

The Budgie (Parakeet) with No Language

My grandmother's budgie, Peetie, had a prolific vocabulary. When he died, the house became ominously quiet. There were no more "Polly want a cracker? What chew doing? Helloooow" or any other tweets to greet you when you entered the living room or walked down the hall.

Grandma bought a new blue budgie that she named Tweetie. She talked to him every day, but Tweetie remained silent.

When I visited that summer, she said, "Tweetie is no Peetie. He is just a dumb bird."

At night I shared the living room with Tweetie and a large grand piano that no one played. My bed was the comfy couch beneath the picture window.

Early in the morning when shadows hide, I was awakened by an unfamiliar noise.

The house was dark, and I lay there on the couch trying to control my racing heart.

The bird wrestled underneath his half-draped cage and erupted in his very first phrase. "Oh-damn-it-why-don't-you-talk.... Oh-damn-it-why-don't-you-talk!"

I learned two lessons that night:
- persistence is often rewarded in strange ways, and —
- my grandmother swore like an intimidating lineman.

It's the Law...

IN AMERICA'S DAIRYLAND in the 1960's, all citizens ate butter. It was the law. To promote the dairy industry, it was illegal in Wisconsin to use oleo in restaurants or to sell colored margarine in the grocery stores.

If colored oleo was the family's choice, there were two options. One-pound colorless, plastic packets of oleo were available complete with a color-generating capsule. To color the margarine required breaking the capsule and kneading the bag into submission. Usually the hands tired before the color mixing was complete, resulting in variegated margarine. The dark streaks were bitter, and the pale patches were bland.

There was a second option, however. Just over the Illinois border, around the first bend in the road, was a series of oleo shacks selling cases of Blue Bonnet, Mazola, and any other product imaginable. You could buy margarine by the stick, by the case, or by the vat.

It was illegal, of course, to bring cases of the yellow stuff across the border, but the highway patrol could not perform a search unless there was "reasonable cause."

I grew up in a small town of thirty thousand people about two hundred miles north of the Illinois line. Wausau had three industries: dairy farms, paper mills, and insurance. The church provided most of the social opportunities for the family. Many churches also provided an oleo service.

Our pastor was required to attend quarterly meetings in Chicago. The week before the meeting there would be an oleo sign-up sheet in the church office. All that was needed was to tell Reverend Nagler what kind and how much, pay up front — and he would deliver.

Small families split cases; larger families bought several. They made wonderful Christmas presents for family and friends in northern Wisconsin who had no reason to go to the Windy City.

At the close of the conference, Reverend Nagler would head home, stopping at his favorite oleo shacks to fill all orders. In the late sixties it was still required that a minister have a stately, black car. Conservative dress was also required.

Reverend Nagler's large black Lincoln matched his straight black hair and his pinstripe suit. He looked more like a gangster than a minister. This connection was enhanced in the collective mind of the Midwest where Dillinger and his cronies were still part of everyday conversation.

Northern Wisconsin lodges still had unpatched bullet holes in the floors — evidence that "Dillinger's gang slept here." Rumors were carried down from father to son concerning the battles that were fought, how many were killed, and where the hideouts were located. Winters are long, and stories may linger longer under such conditions.

But there was no getting around it — Reverend Nagler did look suspicious. Perhaps it was the greased black hair pushed back in a pompadour style. Perhaps it was his stocky build, his sallow complexion, and those dark, piercing eyes. Black was not his color, and he did not wear it well.

One hot July day Reverend Nagler was coming back from Chicago. He had loaded up his black Lincoln with cases and cases of oleo and had crossed the border into Wisconsin.

About fifty miles north of the border, the car internally hemorrhaged and died. He was forced to leave the lifeless hulk by the roadside in the wheat-ripening sun and hike into Sun Prairie, Wisconsin, for help.

Help was not forthcoming until the next day. By the

time the tow truck came, there was more than enough reasonable cause to warrant a search.

The car was standing in a huge pool of melted oleo. Oleo dripped from the differential and coated the tires. Oleo stood in pools in the floor of the back seat and drizzled from the bottom of the back doors.

It must have been an amazing sight.

The highway patrol was duly impressed and fined Reverend Nagler the limit the law would allow.

The collection the next Sunday went to cover Reverend Nagler's fine.

The law has now been changed, and the oleo shacks are gone, but if you are ever eating in a Wisconsin restaurant, take note of that patty that you put on your baked potato — it's butter. It's the law.

Well, It's Happening

TODAY I WATCHED a young bike rider chasing and being chased by cars at the outer edge of a four-lane highway. The well-toned muscles kept in time with my stereo. Not a scratch marred the sinew and muscle of that lithe body. Not a bit of protection was perched on his wind-tossed hair. As I watched in semi-awe and confusion, I realized that I had slipped quietly into middle age.

Not long ago I would have rushed for my bike and searched with him for the wind. Today I only smiled. A few close calls have taught me that I could get killed between the gutter and those cars. A few attempts at dodging a carefully aimed beer can or a carelessly aimed right front tire, and I take the car, not the bike.

When I was young, I did not weigh the course of my actions. It's a good thing I did not. Few middle-aged people would resign a good paying job and take on the costs of graduate school with no money and only the vague hope that if you did well, you might get some support in the future. But at twenty-two, I didn't hesitate. I didn't worry that there were no jobs in the field in which I wanted to study. I didn't worry that if I didn't get support within the year, I would have to leave school. It never dawned on me that things might not work out.

At twenty-two I would go backpacking and hiking alone. I never thought about the cold, the rain, injury, or the things that go wrong at night. Now I worry, and the possibilities of what could go wrong keep me up at night.

Yes, somehow when I wasn't paying any attention, second and third thoughts started to creep into my thinking process. I now worry more about the consequences of my actions, and it has occurred to me more than once that no organism has made it through this world alive.

At this time in my life, I am making decisions based on how I choose to live because I am afraid to die. At twenty-two I made decisions because it looked like fun, life was one great adventure, or it was simply there.

Will old age occur when I'm afraid to do anything because of the consequences? If that's the case, I am heading for my bicycle pump right now.

HOUND TALES

Fleabags

AFTER ENCOUNTERING a leather-clad, chain-carrying motorcycle gang on my last plant-collecting outing, I was somewhat reluctant to venture out collecting alone. The next week, however, proved to be perfect for the quest of new county records. The lure of the unusual out-competed the fear of the wild, and I was off again.

But, just in case, I decided to go armed. I took my dog.

FLEABAGS is a large amalgamation of breeds and although large of frame, she is weak of mind and body. She will come to any of the following endearing terms — Crummy, Crumblicker, Bowinkle, or Liverwurst — that is, as long as there is nothing else that she would rather do, such as stalking garbage and long-dead animals. Upon finding either, she will roll till she is endowed with the proper aroma and then proudly return with her head held high, assured of attracting flies and my attention.

With Fleabags on the front seat, we headed for the woods. Our destination was a point of land called Pinckneyville. The area was near the confluence of two streams, so upon arriving, I was not suspicious at seeing a red sports car with its trunk open. I just assumed that the fishing was good, the lure for the lunker was too great, and a hurrying fisherman had left his trunk open.

I began to collect plants, thinking nothing more of the car or its owner. Crummy loafed off to investigate the smells of Pinckneyville. It was not long before the quiet of the September noon was interrupted by, "You damned dog, come back with our lunch!"

Startled, I looked towards the bushes from which the cry had come. The dense honeysuckle shrubs were strung with all manner of clothing — a shirt here, pants there, and assorted underwear atop it all. Out from under this natural clothesline, Fleabags emerged, tail tucked to her sternum with a large piece of chicken dangling from her mouth and potato salad slipping slowly down her side.

She had interrupted a buff picnic.

Laughing, I removed the pickles and mayonnaise from her hair. The chicken looked good. I almost sent her back for seconds. I didn't notice the baked beans smeared on her ear till we were in the car. There she was, mistress of it all, with beans dripping from her ear.

I learn about as fast as Fleabags, and on my next outing the dog came along. This time we headed for a stream in search of Cardinal Flowers and wild Gentians.

We started up a rocky rivulet, an ideal habitat for these flowers. The woods were lush and green. The water careened over several rocky ridges and zigzagged across the rocky river bed. Quiet pools held Water Striders suspended on the surface, casting their characteristic large footed shadows onto the sandy patches at the bottom of these pools.

But like many picturesque spots in the Carolinas, people had used the area as a gathering spot on long summer evenings. These evening gatherings were liberally doused with liquor and were dedicated to the local tradition of "getting right." After the liquid refreshment was gone, the fun continued by tossing the glass bottles against the rocks. This area was strewn with glass. I discovered it too late. Fleabags had already stepped on a jagged Budweiser bottle. She didn't cry out, and she tried to follow. But the cut was deep, and blood flowed freely. She finally whimpered. She was in trouble.

I scooped her up — all forty pounds — and firmly held the paw above my head to slow the bleeding. The rocks which only moments ago had been fun to hop over were now major obstacles.

Balancing the dog as best I could on my right hip and holding her left paw in the air, I headed back to the truck a half mile away. At times I would lose my footing, and a squirt of blood would arch from the paw to the front of my shirt. The final few yards were vertical, and several times I skidded butt first down to the bottom. Again a new squirt of blood would arch from the gaping wound. On the third or fourth try, I managed to make it to the top. My troubles were not over, however. The truck had a floor mounted gearshift. How was I going to hold the paw, drive, shift, and keep the dog quiet all at the same time?

I tied the dog down with the seat belts. Holding the paw in my right hand, I found I could shift if I held the steering wheel with my chin and shifted with my left. This required a torqueing of the body which left only one eye at best on the road.

I drove forty-five miles through back roads juggling

gears, paws, and pets to soothe a frightened pup. More than one truck driver took a second glance at the mysterious technique being used to get one small truck down the road.

The vet took one look, anesthetized Fleabags, and placed six to eight stitches in her paw.

About halfway through the operation, I remembered an important meeting I had to attend in ten minutes. Dropping the dog at a friend's house, I ran to my meeting, arriving only seven minutes late. It was only after I sat down in the plush chairs of the meeting room at the university that I remembered the blood. I looked down.

There were three Jackson Pollock-like splotches of crimson across my front and a large rosy patch on my side. As a horrified expression crossed over my face, the chair of the committee looked at me and said, "Is it yours, or did you kill someone?"

I replied, "No. It's Fleabag's."

This led to a long, involved explanation — which you already know.

An End and a Beginning
OR
The Changing of the Guards

UPON LOSING my special friend of fourteen years, I was not sure I could or should replace old Crumb-licker / Fleabags / Coco. Her death was unexpected but anticipated. For about six months I had noticed she was slow to rise, and I would catch her staring off into space as if she were unaware of her world or dreaming of better days. At night she was restless and spent much of her time pacing from room to room.

But spring was in the air, and the warmth of a few exceptionally nice days in late February gave her new energy. It was a Friday. Since I had some field plots to check, Crumb-licker and I spent the afternoon in the woods. She ran like a pup and came like a jet-propelled hairball when I called her. She was never good at stopping, and as usual, she used my legs to assist her in the final deceleration. For years she had been troubled with a front shoulder that frequently went out of joint. Twice during the afternoon she came limping back to me in a tripod mode. A quick massage and she would be off again. By the end of the day she was tired, but her afternoon frisk was a joy to see.

In the evening as we usually did, we went down to the neighbors' for dinner. I knew she was tired from the day's romp, and I was not alarmed when I did not see her for a few hours.

At around ten I became suddenly uneasy. We had been talking about nothing at all and certainly not about dogs, but I knew something was dreadfully wrong.

I called her.

She did not come.

No one in the house could remember seeing her. Often she would crawl under a bed and be out of circulation for long periods of time. But no bed covered the brown bomber.

She was not in the house.

It had turned back into winter. There was a cold rain falling.

She always hated the rain.

I walked home hoping she was there. I knew I would never see her alive again. I knew that the inevitable had already happened.

All night long I paced the house and circled the block, calling her name.

Her favorite food was placed on the front step, and her favorite cookies crumbled in my pocket.

By morning the rain had quit but not my pacing.

I walked her favorite walks and stalked her favorite garbage cans. No luck. Finally, I gave up thinking and just let my feet carry me as they would. I left the house and walked a straight line through a patch of woods and drawn, as if by a homing beacon, I crossed a four-lane roadway. There on the far side of the road in a patch of early spring onions lay a brown, distorted lump.

I now knew it all.

Somehow she had gotten out without anyone noticing and headed along one of her favorite routes. She had been running home, perhaps in response to my unuttered call, and had been hit. At least the person who hit her had taken time to lay her in the grass at the road's edge. Her hip was shattered, her leg broken, and a wide gash which had not bled was on that head that I used to pet to start each new day.

It had been quick. She did not have time to bleed.

I don't remember going home or getting her favorite bedding. I do remember picking up my lifeless, wet, matted friend, and placing her for the last time on that old blue bed.

A friend and I drove her to the cabin in the woods where

she loved to run. My friend's dog, Gumpy, went with us. Nothing much was said as we drove west into the mountains.

Because of all the rain, the earth was easy to dig. When the hole was deeper and much wider than it needed to be, I got her from the back of the truck.

The exhaust from the truck had made her body almost warm. For one second I thought that perhaps she was not dead.

But no, that was impossible.

As I carried her to the hole, Gumpy and the black dog, Star, who really owned the mountain, followed slowly behind.

I laid her in the hole and patted her one last time. Her two dog friends sat quietly on the mound of dirt by the grave's edge. As I picked up the shovel to complete the task, both dogs rose, gave the still body one final sniff, and then moved out of the way of the flying dirt. They did not go far. When I stopped to rest, there they were, sitting side by side, watching every shovel of dirt as it covered up their lifeless friend.

After completing the task, I went and sat for a while on the wooden steps of the cabin. Both dogs sat quietly by my side. It was a sunny day. The woods were quiet. Spring would be here soon.

The rest of the weekend was a blur. Monday came, and I threw myself into work, making any excuse not to go home. Perhaps a trip to the pound was the cure. Perhaps I could find an animal that needed me as much as I needed her. I walked down row after row of cages looking for a cocoa brown female hound with sparkling eyes.

There was no Crumb-licker the second.

I was ready to leave. Too many dogs, but not that special one to replace my old friend.

The attendant was bringing in a particularly unruly animal, and I stepped out of the way to make his job easier. In so doing, I stopped next to a cage that held the most miserable dog I had ever seen. He was all wrong. He was long-haired, blond, male, and oh, so timid.

I bent down to comfort him. His nose just lay in my hands. As I petted him, he began to lean on me, and his tail moved ever so slowly.

"You really are a poor lost soul," I said.

His large, matted, brown eyes blinked in response.

I looked at the card tacked to his cage. A bold pen had written ***"scared"*** in large letters across the card. As if that were not enough, he had diarrhea.

I got up to leave. The nose continued to lie in my hands. Dropping my head, I turned to go. He slowly got to his feet and tried to follow. I returned to the cage. If ever a dog needed help, this was the dog.

I left to get the attendant and make arrangements.

All the way home he just sat on the front seat. He showed no interest in his surroundings and even less interest in where he was going.

We made one stop at the vet's for shots and medication, and home we went.

Upon getting into the house, he went to the rug I had given him in the kitchen and did not move for three days — that is, except to take care of emergencies caused by the diarrhea.

He did not know how to walk on a leash. He did not react to anything. He just lay on his rug and ate very little. Gradually, his appetite increased, and his interest in his surroundings improved, as did his general physical condition.

In a week he would walk around the block if it was not garbage day. Garbage bags were something too frightening to be passed. If we got within fifty feet of one of those black monsters, he would become prostrate and begin to shake. I had to pick him up and carry him around the black monster.

Men in baseball caps created the same reaction. He would cower, shake, and try to flee. His stock response for anything new was no response. All motions were slow, and he would eat only when no one was around.

His reactions and movements resembled an uncertain amoeba. When he got off the couch, which was not often, he flowed off and onto the floor. Any unnecessary movement was always avoided.

There was pathos in every move. He had only two speeds — no and slow.

The name came early on in our trial period. It was an obvious choice for anyone whose favorite TV show was M*A*S*H. His name was O'Riley (Riley, for short) after Walter O'Reilly, who had many of the same personality traits.

Riley it is. We have learned to ooze through life together. There is nothing exuberant about him, except maybe his love for soft, expensive things. These are rendered into soft piles of confetti with un-Riley like speed. Alas, I have never seen these energy spurts — only the results. He can devour a chair within the time it takes to go to the store for a paper.

Yesterday I left for less than five minutes. When I returned, I found the living room looking as if a freak snowstorm had occurred. There was Riley in the middle of a foot deep layer of little tiny Styrofoam balls. The amoeba had attacked a beanbag chair, and for once, the amoeba had won.

A Dog with an Alias

Sex: Male
Name: MacDuff, alias Spot, alias Stray
Born: December, 1995, under the Kentucky Fried Chicken, Simpsonville, SC
Description: Basset x Terrier
    Brown/white blotched, wiry hair
    37 pounds
    1.5 feet high, 4 feet long
History: 8 months no-kill animal shelter
Adoption 1: One day to a family with a small baby
Reason for Return: Territorial dispute with baby
Adoption 2: July 15, 1996, to Newberry
Reason for Return: Many — Date to be decided
Attitude: Yes
Hobbies: Chewing up egg cartons, cardboard boxes, barking

A DOG WITH AN ALIAS is not the easiest thing to befriend. Mac has certainly lived up to this statement. Why he is still with us is hard to say. After destroying one love seat, three rugs, and one door; after repeatedly decorating the den with smelly offal; and after waging vocal territorial battles with Molly (an eight-pound black pug-pick) and Mary, my housemate, he is definitely approaching the abyss.

    If destruction were not enough, he also has an underwear fetish. Socks are pulled from feet and carried through the dog door into the back yard. Underwear, if dropped during changing, will accompany the socks into the light of day. The yard must be surveyed before guests arrive, or when metermen or repairmen are expected.

A bath cannot be taken in solitude. The door is no deterrent. Mac will just barrel through, perch on the tub, and watch. Dripping faucets fascinate him, as well as right shoulders. Since he has come to rule, my right shoulder has a decidedly different texture than my left. Mac's tongue is better than a loofah sponge.

It's not just baths but all bathroom activities that attract him. As soon as I get myself perched, there he is, sitting on my left foot and looking up with a distinctive roll of the eyes as if to say, "Don't you want to pet me?"

Right now he is sprawled in the middle of the now fringeless Oriental carpet de-corrugating a cardboard box. A once sizeable box is being noisily rendered into moist, thumbnail sized pieces. We cope with this by carpeting most of the house in mottled-brown carpet.

The Mary-Mac wars are harder to deal with. Both combatants are stubborn and hate strange, repetitive noises. Mac's response is predictable. He will cock his head and bark and groan and squeal. Mary's reply will be one or more of the following:

"I hate you, dog."

"I've never liked you."

"Oh, shut up!"

"Damn you, dog!"

"If I had somewhere to go, I would leave."

Mac will respond with an eye roll. Molly will look on smugly from the couch. But if Mac seeks my support, Molly will attack — bounce over the coffee table and into Mac with a flurry of high-pitched squeals, frequently ending up on Mac's chest, panting furiously.

Mac rolls his eyes at me. "What did I do?" he seems to plead.

"Oh, shut up!" chimes in Mary.

What possible joy could be found in this scene? Being a dog lover would help. But at night, after a trying day at the Mary-Mac/Molly-Mac wars, a quietness settles into the living room. Molly sleeps contentedly next to me on the couch. Mac rests under the coffee table, squeezed into an ex-Molly bed which is much too small for him. Parts of him dangle limply onto the carpet. Mary sits in the shabby remains of a once elegant, red love seat with patches of white stuffing sticking out of the Mac-attacked arms.

A peace descends upon the household.

I pet Molly with one hand and rub Mac with my left foot. Both utter contented sighs, and Mac rolls his eyes. This holds until a branch taps on the window, a siren wails, a dog barks, or a train whistle whines in the night. Then the whole scenario is played out again with little variation in sound or fury.

M%%AC IS NOW%% 427 days, almost 428 days old. Only 215 days until maturity will moderate the frequency and intensity of the skirmishes. Molly will have been quieted by middle age, and we will have saved up enough money to refurnish the house with a visit to Rooms to Go.

Symbiosis

As soon as I enter the driveway, I hear the barking. Moments before, they were lying in a patch of sun contemplating the digestion of their morning meal or quietly inspecting the passage of an ant column. Now they were vying for a space on the dog deck and racing to be the first one into the doggy door.

By the time I am out of the car, I hear the vinyl flap slam, and the squealing and yapping commence. As I mount the stairs, a low snuffling sound begins, and a parade of nose shadows moves back and forth beneath the crack at the bottom of the closed kitchen door.

The door pushes open, and two mongrels look down at me, squealing with delight and vying for the first pet.

It is with judicious precision that I make contact with both of them at the same time. Otherwise, there is a growl and a push as Molly, the smaller black Pekingese mix, is pushed to the back by the terrible terrier mix that is Mac.

After the initial greeting there is a rush to the kitchen for their afternoon treat. Both sit in rapt attention, staring at the golden retriever-shaped cookie jar that holds their toasted mini-wheat snacks.

The routine is unvarying. The path to the jar precise. The number of cookies doled out counted.

Only then can I check my mail or attend to making a cup of tea. I am home. The ritualistic greeting is much more important than any cup of tea.

Mac and Molly warm an empty house. It is a routine that provides framework for life at home.

It does not end with a wheat biscuit. It pervades the whole day from breakfast to the ceremonial trip to the back yard at 11:05 PM, which is always followed by two pretzel bits and a pet. It orchestrates and provides structure to my life.

Molly's perch on the couch and Mac's bed beneath the coffee table are within reach of a hand or a foot should I need to feel the warmth of a friend.

Yes, four-footed, wet-nosed, curly-haired, brown-eyed, tail-wagging friends.

I need them more than they need me. It's a symbiosis of souls. It is a mutualism between two species for the benefit of both.

COULD THEY live without me? Probably. Could I live without them? Probably not.

The Dog No One Wanted

FOUR OWNERS had tried to live with him.... His exuberance and barking commentary proved to be too problematic. There was no doubt that he was bright, friendly, but oh, so strong-willed.

He had been found playing with children in a schoolyard and was named after the school mascot, The Griffin. The love of children was a defining trait. Every time he heard children at play, he would run to them.

He noisily guarded anyone who would be his master. Neighbors objected, and a new master was quickly found.

I live at the edge of an expansive woods in a neighborhood defined by four-acre lots arranged about a picturesque lake. My household usually includes several dogs, but I was now down to a golden Jack Russell mix named Sassafras.

She took to Griffin on an introductory walk about the lake.

It was settled; my menagerie had expanded by one.

I had successfully introduced him to the dog door and had gone into the bathroom. Griffin followed. When he smelled my output, he squatted at my feet and produced one of his own.

How do you handle that!

I picked it up, went out into the back yard, and placed it prominently in the middle of the largest grassy spot.

He got the message, and further deposits he offered were placed in the center of that grassy patch.

He loves the walks and anticipates the outings. If we have not started the process by five in the afternoon, he goes into spasms of barking. Sassafras joins in. The intensity of the prancing and barking continues until I succumb and grab the leash.

My neighbors love golf carts and ride their dogs around the lake on their daily outings. Some even put their dogs on dog leashes and accompany them around the lake on their carts.

Griffin thinks these barking carts are invading his territory. Frantic barking results. I have gotten him to sit as the carts go by, but the furious barking spasms are not that easily corrected.

I have tried water pistols, pennies shaken in a tin can, shock collars, whistles, collars that produce a high pitch, and verbal abuse. Nothing has worked. He has even taught Sassafras the art of golf cart defense.

He is jealous of the phone and vocally comments throughout the conversation.

Despite all this, the three of us are inseparable. We sleep together, watch TV together, and one is always a book prop when I read. Our lives are entwined and enriched by each other. Griffin is more than a watchdog; he monitors my physical state.

I am an insulin dependent diabetic. Over the past years my blood sugar levels have dropped during the night.

When this first happened, I was aroused by Griffin's frantic barking. I was shaking and could not walk. I rolled to the floor and grabbed Griffin's collar. He helped me to the kitchen where I could get some juice from the fridge.

Now I keep honey packets by my bed. When Griffin wakes me, all I have to do is reach for the packets close at hand. Griffin is my service dog, while Sassafras just sleeps right through the episode.

The shock collars and water guns are put away. I will scold him for his excesses, but without him, tomorrow is far less certain.

Dodge

IT WAS a cool Saturday morning in early fall. Like most people, I had errands to run. The luxury of the day was encapsulated in the knowledge that the stores didn't open until 10:00. I nestled down under the covers and took another two-hour nap.

A quick non-fat bologna sandwich for breakfast, one of my staples in life, and I was on my way. As I left the back door, the young hawk I had watched mature throughout the summer soared overhead. The mewing cries were pleasingly familiar. I looked up to catch its tail as it disappeared over the tops of the oak tree at the crest of the hill.

As I started the car, the mewing continued.

"He must have caught an updraft," I thought.

Crossing the dam, I looked for the hawk above the tree line. He had slipped over the ridge and was gone. The hawk had moved on, but the mewing sound was getting louder and louder. As I turned onto Mansfield, I suddenly realized that the sound was not coming from above but from under the hood of my mini-van.

I abruptly stopped the van in the middle of the road and turned off the engine. Quickly, I ran, opened the hood, and peered into the engine compartment. I know nothing about the normal sounds a car should make, let alone any mews.

I listened. At first there was silence, then a woeful mew. It was coming from the bowels of the compartment.

I was crawling under the car when Harry, a neighbor, pulled up in his mini-van and parked directly behind me.

"Something wrong?" he queried.

"I'm not sure. There seems to be a mewing sound coming from under my hood."

We listened in silence for almost a minute until the sound erupted from the bowels of the engine. "MEW, MEW, MEW-MEW."

"It's a cat," he said emphatically.

"But where?"

He crawled into the engine compartment, and I crawled in beside him. Now there were two pairs of feet sticking out from under the hood of a blue van angularly parked in the middle of the street.

Marge, another neighbor, was in her mini-van when she spied the unusual scene. She stopped, parked her mini-van at the back of the line, and got out to help.

We explained the situation. Now there were three sets of feet, two pairs sticking out from under the hood and one pair poking out from behind the left front tire.

"There it is!" Marge cried from above.

"Where?" I said from below.

"Sitting on top of the shock absorber."

As I focused on the area, I could just make out two blue orbs surrounded by black. Some of the black was natural and some was mini-van grease.

My hand would fit, but my arms were too short.

Harry's arm was long enough, but it wouldn't fit. Marge's arm was just right. Stretching to her full length, she could just get the cat by the scruff of the neck.

There she was, a kitty too small to be weaned from its mother. Marge placed it in my hands, and suddenly my neighbors were gone.

Where a moment ago three mini-vans had been parked, only one remained. I was alone with a new kitten.

I don't like cats.

It was cute, though, and oh, so small. Her eyes were bright, and beneath the grease showed a multi-colored coat that appeared in good condition. There was no blood.

I got into the bucket seat, perching the kitten on my left shoulder. The circle drive led right back to my front door.

"Mary, we have a problem," I yelled, as I entered the front door. Mary is my housemate.

"No, WE don't," she replied.

"What can I do with it?"

"Well, it can't stay here. We already have three dogs, a cat, and an opossum. We don't need another cat."

She was right.

"Besides," she went on, "my cat is allergic to the leukemia vaccination. If that cat has leukemia, Kitty will get it."

Right again. Now what?

I left, clutching the small thing in my hands. Only two blue orbs peered out at me. "I'll take it to the vet's to see if she's hurt. That's the least I can do," I said to myself. The vet was only three miles away, but by the time I got there, I liked cats even less. She had scratched me, climbed over my head, and had wedged herself in the most inaccessible corner of the van. It was only with much effort and blood loss that I got her into the vet's office.

Debbie, our vet, checked her over. "She would clean up fine," she said. The grease was the only evidence of her ordeal.

"Do you know of anyone that has just lost a cat and needs and wants a kitty?" I asked.

"No," was the reply. "You could take her to the shelter, but they won't take a cat unless it's over two pounds."

"Dodge" (what else would you name a cat that materialized out of a Dodge Caravan?) was well under the two-pound limit.

Now what?

Finally, the vet agreed to keep her over the weekend if I would look for a home for her. She would look too. Maybe the problem would resolve itself soon.

Monday came, and I had called every cat lover I knew. They had either sworn off cats or had their fill. I was in the departmental office pouring my third cup of coffee when

Joyce, our secretary, said, "How was your weekend?"

I told her about Dodge.

"Well, you should have asked me," she said. "I would have taken her."

I ran to the phone and dialed the vet's.

"Have you got a home for Dodge yet?" I asked.

"No," was the reply.

"Well, I have!" I said triumphantly. "Joyce, our secretary, wants her." We arranged for the pickup and it was over.

UPDATE: Dodge was not an agreeable housepet. She spat and pounced whenever Joyce entered a room, and she initiated battles with Joyce's older cat, Cuddles.

One day Dodge streaked out of the house and into a neighboring vacant lot. No search was made. No bowl of warm milk was offered.

Is He Dead Yet?

UNCLE BILL was suffering from Alzheimer's when his dog, Rusty, died. He could no longer walk him, and a new dog was not an option.

Someone suggested a cat.

My aunt, who was seventy-two at the time, was working as a designated driver for a local Dodge dealership. She asked at work if anyone knew where she could get a cat.

"Sure," said one of the mechanics, "I'll bring you one tomorrow."

True to his word, he presented Aunt Lee with a black cat quietly resting in a cat carrier.

All the way home the cat remained motionless and appeared to be not the least bothered by his change of venue.

We brought the cat carrier into the study and gently opened the cage.

At first, the cat did not move. Then, seemingly under jet propulsion, he leaped from the carrier and within seconds, the old paper window shades were confetti. The curtains soon followed. He bolted from the room and disappeared.

Prying and prodding into every corner of the house proved useless. All we could do was lay out food and water next to the litter box in the kitchen and go to bed.

Late that night I heard a mournful mewing and tried to trace its origin, but finding a black cat on a dark night was impossible.

For several days the pattern remained the same. The cat

would prowl through the house during the night and hide during the day — that is, until my aunt opened the refrigerator and a clump of cat dropping careened off her head and into the gravy she was setting on the refrigerator shelf.

"That dammed cat," was all she said.

Every morning my uncle still drove his truck down to the Owl's Lodge where he had lunch, had a drink with the boys, and "signed the Book." These trips became shorter and shorter as his disease progressed. All he said was he didn't know any of the guys any more.

On the morning of the fallen turd, my uncle entered the house, placed his coat on the same hook he had been using for sixty years, and said, "Is he dead yet?"

The cat had a name.

It took us over a week to corral the cat behind the commode and box him for his return to his former owner.

When my aunt handed the carrier back to the mechanic, he said, "Well, he was just a barn cat," and he guessed he didn't know about litter boxes.

My uncle still missed Rusty.

The family persuaded Aunt Lee to try the animal shelter.

Both my uncle and aunt went. As they entered the facility, a gray cat was lying on the counter purring happily at the pets from strangers. A bond seemed to be struck between the gray feline and my uncle. He called her Kitty.

Kitty loved to sit on my uncle's lap and slept on the foot of his bed. Every time my uncle sat in the overstuffed recliner, Kitty would materialize, curl up on his lap, and purr to my uncle's touch.

The disease continued to progress. Uncle Bill had been a powerful man and still weighed over two hundred pounds. My aunt cared for him as long as she could and longer than she should. But she could not lift him and was forced to place him in a wonderfully caring nursing home.

She visited him three times a day and had dinner with him most evenings.

One day she thought that Bill would like to see Kitty.

She corralled the cat, placed her in a carrier, and took her to the care facility. She gently took the cat out of the cage and placed her on Uncle Bill's lap.

They both looked at each other as if they were strangers. He no longer recognized the cat, and Kitty did not seem to know the frail man in the wheelchair.

My uncle is gone now, but Kitty still prowls the halls of the house at night. It's as if she is still looking for her old pal, Bill.

Tales and Trails of a Botany Professor

There Is Safety in Numbers

As an undergraduate at the University of Wisconsin, I found it hard to get the professor's attention. Often we were in classes with 200–700 other students. We existed on the rolls and in the grade book as a series of numbers. No one knew our names. If we met our professor in the hall, he would not even know that we were in his class.

But if we chose a small discipline and enrolled in junior and senior level classes, the numbers of students thinned to 30–75/class.

As upper class students, we could live off campus. Housing was cheaper and much quieter than the dorms. The downside was the commute.

I lived in a garret apartment overlooking Lake Mendota. In the summer I would bike to school, but in winter I ice-skated across the lake. The southwest wind would sweep the lake clear of snow, leaving only snow patches and ice ridges to add challenges to the trip.

Each morning I would walk to the lake edge, strap on my skates, shove my shoes in a backpack, and I was off. It was fun avoiding the cracks, riding the ridges, and skating around the multi-armed patches of snow, but it was always unpredictable. Depending on the number of obstacles to be avoided, the skate could take from twenty to forty minutes.

One day I was late. A new pair of skates had been time consuming to get on and laced properly. I was forced to try taking some shortcuts. I jumped over snow patches and soared over jagged cracks in the ice. This was fun, and all went well for a while, until I tried to jump a half hidden crack and got my skate caught in the very jagged end of the crevice. Down I went, but the bruised knees were soon forgotten when I realized that my new skate was hopelessly caught in the ice. I moved my foot back and forth, tilting it, but the blade remained firmly encased in the ice. I tried to thaw the ice with my hand but only managed to get my hand frozen to the skate. Desperate now, I removed both skates and used one as an ice pick to free the second. After an inordinately long time, the skate slipped free.

Rebooting, I raced to the Student Union. Usually I checked my skates in a locker and wore my shoes to class.

No time. I put back on my land boots, tied the strings of the skates together, threw them over my left shoulder, and ran up Bascom Hill to my favorite professor's botany class.

I did so want to impress Dr. Clark. The class was small, only about sixty students, but it was a good group.

As I neared the classroom, I looked at my watch. I was ten minutes late. The door was shut. It was one of those old wooden doors with the upper half inset with a large pane of opaque glass. The room number, 320, was printed at the top center of the glass in black paint.

I eased the door open, went in, and closed the door quietly behind me.

So far, so good. The room was longer than wide. The blackboard ran along the long wall to my right. As I started to move to my left to take a seat, the skates slipped. I caught them and threw them back over my shoulder. One of the skate tips hit the door glass, and it shattered.

Dr. Clark stopped, looked slowly over to the shattered door, and peered over his glasses. "I thought it was you," he said.

I lowered my head and, speaking more to my shoes than to Dr. Clark, I said, "I'm sorry I'm late. I got my skate caught in the ice." Never looking up, I made my way to the back of the class.

After this I was determined to prove to Dr. Clark that I

was something other than a klutz, but the more I tried, the worse it got.

On field trips I tried to stay as close to him as possible. Frequently, I would get behind and had to run to catch up. Running in the woods only led to tripping. After one of my many trips, Dr. Clark commented, "You are the clumsiest student I have ever taken to the woods."

"Damn it," I said under my breath. "I'll show him." I practiced running, walking, and walking stealthily in the woods, but the fieldwork was over before I mastered it.

Final exams came. The ice melted. I rode my bike the two miles to school each day. Madison is very hilly. Two miles meant two hills to climb between home and school.

I had overslept and was late for Dr. Clark's class.

"Not again," I moaned.

With an adrenalin assist I flew over the first hill and raced down the other side. As I passed a row of parked cars, someone opened a door. All I saw was a blur of metal.

I swerved.

The bike went one way and I caromed off the door, over the hood, and crumpled onto the pavement.

Dazed, I got to my feet.

Mumbling, "I'll be back. I've got a test to take," I grabbed my slightly bent bike and headed up Bascom Hill to Birge Hall and my date with Dr. Clark.

Slamming the bike into the rack, I noticed that my right arm was bleeding. "Good thing I'm left-handed," I muttered and wrapped my scarf about the offending arm.

I ran to room 320, on time.

By the end of the test, I couldn't remember my name. When I moved stiffly to the front to turn in my blue book, I noticed it was covered with blood.

When I handed the book to Dr. Clark, he looked up questioningly. "Are you all right?" he asked.

I said I had had a bit of a bike accident on my way to class and would probably go over to the emergency room and get checked out.

Dr. Clark took me.

I was diagnosed with a mild concussion and a broken arm.

They kept me overnight.

When I stopped by Dr. Clark's office to get my grade, he asked me to come in and sit down.

"What now?" I wondered under my breath.

Dr. Clark handed me the blood-stained blue book. I looked down at it and noted in the left-hand corner a red 100 with a circle around it.

"I've never had a student get a hundred on this test in all my twenty years of teaching," he said.

That was the only 100 I ever got as an undergraduate at the University of Wisconsin.

Cows and Nettles

I HAD READ about stinging nettles, *Urtica dioica*. I had even intentionally touched a few of the hollow hairs on the stems and leaves, which contain oxalic acid. When brushed, these hairs puncture the skin, break, and release the acid into the wound. The sting is immediate and lasts as long as an hour or more. The area affected becomes red and puffy, but I had never experienced total body emergence until one fatal day by a Wisconsin stream.

I WAS DOING FIELDWORK for my Master's degree. The temperature was well over one hundred, and there was no breeze. I had been in the field collecting lichens all morning when I came upon a small stream. The water was cool and deep. Clear, sandy-bottomed pools offered instant relief from the heat. The woods appeared lifeless. I stripped off my hot field clothes and waded into the stream. A large boulder in the center provided a perfect perch. It's hard to know how long I sat there dangling my feet in the refreshing pool.

Suddenly, the sound of a tuneless whistle and the plop-plop of cows entering the water splintered the silence. Upstream of me, a large herd of cattle was being driven across the stream and into the woods to escape the heat. Whenever cows get near water, they tend to relieve themselves. Small to middling sized brown cow patties were beginning to float by.

I was trespassing.

I slipped into the water.

The stream gently bent into the woods, and I floated around the curve and out of sight of the farmer. I crawdaddied my way along, bumping knees and other body parts on submerged rocks. After rounding the bend, I lodged myself between a jumble of rocks and looked about.

No cows, no homes, no farmers. The woods were mature, with thick undergrowth. I floated down around another bend for good measure. The stream bent back to where my car was hidden.

Rounding the river bend, I could hear traffic. Looking downstream, I saw a bridge. Two little boys were fishing from the top arch of the span.

Rising from the water, I turned tail and rushed in a direct line for my clothes. Cutting across the river bend, I ran directly into a large patch of *Urtica dioica*. I was in the middle of it before the pain struck. There was no turning back. The pain was excruciating. I tried not to yell, but the discomfort was beyond silence.

The farmer looked up. His mouth fell open, but he said not a word. The cows were unimpressed.

I grabbed my clothes and dressed on the run to my car.

By the time I got home, my eyes were swelling shut, and red welts covered my body. The burning and dermatitis lasted over a week. The humiliation lasted much longer.

An Invigorating Experience

FOR YEARS I have been allured by woodlands braided by rocky streams. Upon moving to the suburbs of a rapidly metastasizing Southern town, the vertically sloped woods behind my house have rekindled a childhood yen for exploration.

The slopes were too steep to lumber, and the soil was too rocky to farm. As I wandered through this acreage, I discovered two populations of plants on the federally endangered species list. Vertical cascades of Mountain Laurel drooped to the edge of a rapidly flowing, rock bottomed stream.

My search took me into the stream valleys to the north where the ruins of an old gristmill, stone dam, and millpond were losing a battle with Kudzu. Only with great effort could I find that these were the remains of Martin's Mill built around the time of the Civil War.

With each exploratory journey, I found more plant diversity and natural beauty in Peter's Creek and its tributary, Mineral Springs Creek.

The land was owned by a consortium that had plans for a golf course with mini-mansions nestled on the top of these *Kalmia*-clad bluffs. The area, however, was too remote from the high-paying jobs that could have funded such a dream.

The only new residences were of beavers that had built several dams at the confluence of the two creeks. In so doing, they had created a sizable wetland, a rarity in the dissected terrain of the Piedmont.

An eight-year discussion ensued between the developer and the Heritage Trust of South Carolina, eventually culminating in the acquisition of a 162-acre preserve. But there was no money for the development of trails or public interest in such development. I finally got permission to build hiking trails throughout the preserve. We used many preexisting trails, some carved by deer, and others created by the would-be developers who showed prospective clients around the upland on golf carts.

Many people helped. Local colleges got involved, as well as a number of wildlife action groups, Scouts, and people who would listen to my dream.

When I was asked, "What do you want for Christmas?" I would answer, "a half-day of trail building."

Within eight months we had carved four miles of trail. The major problems were the stream crossings. There was no money for bridges.

One day I spied a sack of Redi-Mix Concrete that had been left out in the rain.

"Why not make stepping stones by placing intact bags of Redi-Mix Concrete in the stream? They would conform to the irregular surface of the rock bottomed stream and provide a flat foot fall area."

A group of students rearranged the rocks to provide a stable base for the bags. A protracted drought had made this manageable. My old backpack worked well for carrying the forty-pound bags of mix down the slopes to the stream. Several people assisted, but much of the toting rested on my shoulders.

The nearest access point for my truck was a quarter of a mile away from the stream crossing.

When the wildlife officer in charge of the preserve came to see what we had accomplished, he was amazed. He even provided more concrete mix for our efforts. However, he replaced the forty-pound bags with sixty-pound sacks.

For a five foot one light-framed female, these were a challenge.

One cold but clear Saturday, I decided to try my technique out on these larger bags.

The approach to my parking area was blocked by trucks. A fiber optic cable was being laid along the power line right of way, and my access was blocked.

I parked on the far side of the line of white trucks and proceeded to maneuver a sack into the pack. An awkward moment arose when I tried to settle the heavy pack into a somewhat secure position. The result was not perfect. The pack lay a bit sidewise across my shoulders, and the sack of Redi-Mix clearly showed above the frame.

As I passed the work crew, they were sitting on their tailgates having lunch.

I nodded but said nothing.

They responded in kind.

The pack was not well centered. I had to lean precariously into the hill as I descended to the stream crossing.

A recent rain had increased the water depth of the rock crossing, making some of the approach rocks slippery and increasing the flow rate considerably. The sacks were needed in the very center of the stream.

As I took my second step, my foot slipped. The unbalanced load toppled me backward into the stream. The river was running beneath my armpits, and the backpack was rapidly filling with water.

All I could think of was, "If I died in this position, the person who found me would think that floating down a rocky Piedmont stream with sixty pounds of concrete strapped to one's back was a very odd way to commit suicide."

I tried to lift myself and the pack — impossible.

The water was cold. I was losing strength rapidly.

Eventually, I figured out a backward crawl technique that stabilized the pack on a rock and allowed me to leverage it into the desirable position.

Wiggling out of the straps required me to sink deeper into the cascading pool. After several tries, the pack was on the desired rock, and I was facing it. With one final burst of energy, I freed the pack. It was covered with mud and soaking wet.

There was a bit of a breeze. Chill bumps the size of Mount Rushmore covered exposed surfaces of my body.

After a brief recovery period, I wrung out my shirt, shouldered the dripping pack, and started slowly up the hill to my truck.

As I neared the power line, I stopped to tidy myself a bit. My boots were caked with mud, and mud splashes extended to my waist.

I dumped as much water as I could out of the pack and repositioned it, now empty and containing a splotched mud design with patches of orange bleeding through. Water was still dripping from assorted points as I crossed the power line cut.

The workers were still eating lunch.

Their eyes followed my every move.

As I neared two men on a tailgate, I muttered, "Invigorating."

I could see them mentally questioning my sanity.

"I'll bet," was the only reply.

When I got home, my housemate, Mary, met me at the base of the stairs.

"Don't say a word," I said.

"What?"

"Don't say a word," I repeated.

I removed my boots and wet socks, pulled my shirt-tail out before I removed the mud-patterned pants. After mounting the stairs, I turned left down the hall with as much dignity as I could manage.

As I closed the door to my room I said, "Don't ask, and I won't have to tell you any lies."

A Terminal Addiction

PLANT COLLECTING is an addiction. I have had this problem for some years now. One whole room of my house is overgrown with dry specimens waiting for their proper binomial signature. The room was overflowing well before the addiction got to the critical stage. That occurred last fall. The major symptom of the tertiary stage of this disease is the obsession for new county records. A week is without merit to a person in the later addictive stages if there is no plant discovered which has never before been recorded in that particular county.

My schedule at the university was such last fall that Tuesdays were free to pursue my search for the unusual. All too often it turned out that the unusual had little to do with plants.

My first free Tuesday dawned crystal clear, which was not unusual as we were in the midst of a severe drought. But I felt this was a good omen. After taking care of a few chores, the plant press was stuffed and cinched, and I was off in search of unsampled granite outcrops.

A talk with a local forest ranger directed me to a large escarpment just west of town. The directions were specific: 2.9 miles west, turn right onto a gravel road underneath a power line, and drive to the crest of the second hill.

The turn was no problem. The road, however, was indistinguishable from the clover carpeting the right of way. I passed through weeds that quickly closed over the tracks left by my truck.

"Just follow the power line," kept echoing in my questioning mind.

Then the weeds parted, and my truck and I were on a large expanse of granite dotted with blooming plants.

I was ecstatic. Here were more county records than a botanist had a right to dream of. In my normal, hysterical way I ran from county record to county record, overcome by the diversity and sheer beauty of the place. There were Yuccas, *Opuntia*, Blackberry Lily, and grasses I had never seen before.

As I picked and pressed, I became aware of the sound of motorcycles in the distance. I paid no attention. With the gas crisis the sound was becoming more and more common. The varoom of the engines kept getting louder. Still I was too involved with the sea of grass and the blooms to worry.

Over the rise came the most stereotypical motorcycle gang I had ever seen — complete with leather jackets and chains.

Still I was not alarmed. After all they had as much right to be on the right of way as I. My only gut feeling was that they were riding over county records. How crass! I held my tongue. Few people understand the reaction of a plant collector in the terminal stage of the addiction. It is not probable that one was to find such understanding from individuals riding the ridges of South Carolina in chains and jackboots.

I breathed a sigh of relief. They were moving on. But... no, the last man in line circled and slowed to a stop. He was the largest member of the group. He looked my way and slowly headed for the bushes. I tried not to notice. But a three-hundred-pound bear of a man on a lone outcrop dressed in leather is hard not to notice.

My hope was that he was visiting Mother Nature and would mount and ride off my rocky world. I continued to collect but began to ease ever nearer my truck.

He was interested in nature too — but it was the baser kind. He walked around and came out of the woods not twenty yards from where I was collecting a beautiful specimen of Prickly Pear Cactus. Before I had taken two steps, he had tackled my left leg.

I was mad.

As I turned on my back, I yelled, "Here, hold this!"

Instinctively, he held out both hands. I raised the cactus high over my head and drove the spines into his outstretched palms.

His mouth opened and a stream of words sputtered forth. Only half of these did I really understand, but I wasn't really listening. I was running for my truck.

Thank God the keys were still in it — or were they?

As I neared the driver's side, I could see them dangling from the steering wheel. "Oh thank you, God of the Granite Outcrops!"

Throwing the truck into gear, I drove along the power line right of way, searching frantically for my almost hidden tracks. I looked ever so briefly in my rear view mirror. He was still there. His mouth was moving and expelling a stream of verbiage. He was no longer interested in pursuit. He was sitting on the crest of the outcrop picking thorns out of his paws.

As I descended into the weeds, I was not quite sure of the way, but I was very sure it made little difference.

Out of the Jaws of a Cow

I HAVE BEEN inventorying the endangered plant species of South Carolina for over twenty years. It never fails. The Wildlife Department requests a survey only during the hottest and most humid months. The project is always on the most precipitous cliffs, hottest rock outcrops, or most humidity-laden wetland. The remaining wilds of the Carolinas are carefully guarded by briers, blackberry thickets, stands of Multiflora Rose and copperheads.

Much of my time has been spent searching in the wetlands of Greenville County for Bunched Arrowhead *(Sagittaria fasciculata)*, a federally endangered species. In the seepage springs of the Upstate grow a large assortment of bloodletting plants. Huge greenbriers with half-inch long curved thorns and arching entwined stems guard every depression.

Greenbrier is insidious. Its green stems blend with the foliage and attack when one steps into the soft mud near the base of the multi-stemmed clumps. Yet every town in which I've lived has had an upscale subdivision, townhouse complex or yuppy mall named after this plant. If the developers only knew a little botany, they would surely pick a better moniker.

Last summer my project was to reevaluate all known Bunched Arrowhead populations in an effort to identify the most stable populations. A protracted three-year drought had dried up many wetlands and had put this already endangered plant at even greater risk. Less than thirty populations of Bunched Arrowhead were known in all of South Carolina. All occur within five miles of Travelers Rest. This is a sleepy sounding burg, but in reality, it is in one of the fastest growing regions of the state. Farms are being converted into ten-acre mini-estates with lush John Deere grazing zones. Golf courses are now more common than peach orchards. White board fences and trailers dot the landscape. Wetlands have been transformed into verdant quagmires by the drought.

These seeps that contain the *Sagittaria* plants are unique in many ways. The hydrated muck that supports good populations of Bunched Arrowhead does not support the weight of a human, even a small one. The vegetation surrounding them is always thick and thorny. Old barbed wire fences are lying in wait in every thicket. On a South Carolina summer day there is no breeze, and the ninety-degree heat and matching humidity allow sweat to pool in your hair and cascade from your armpits. The salty water finds every wound inflicted by the blackberries, briers, and thorny roses and makes one acutely aware of even the most minute abrasion. Long pants and sleeves are a must. This combined with the heat makes these areas bearable only in the early morning hours. By one o'clock these wetlands steam.

In the past I have always worked alone, but now that I am an insulin dependent diabetic, I am reluctant to enjoy these places by myself. Hiring students as assistants has become a necessity. In the age of air conditioning and laboratory-dominated science projects, few students apply. Kyle, my assistant on this project, is as Southern as grits. A long drawl punctuates every sentence. He is an excellent worker and has a wonderful eye for spotting plants. We have worked together for several years now, and having Kyle on a project is like putting on a good pair of boots. He seems to increase the efficiency of each trip.

Our directions to the old populations of Bunched Arrowhead read, "0.4 miles from bridge on Road 276." No compass points or details of which side of the bridge were included in the report. The stream on both sides of the bridge was braided with seeps. In order to locate the population, we had to follow each trickle for the prescribed 0.4 of a mile in both directions. Cattle had access to the streambed, creating a mosaic of moist cow pies throughout the drainage.

With clipboard in hand, I took the lead. Kyle followed, lugging a bucket with the blue plastic tape we used to mark viable seeps and the steel tape for measuring the size of the population. The going was easier in the stream and cooler, too.

I trudged ahead and was about two hundred feet upstream of Kyle when I heard a strange sucking sound. Kyle's footfalls ceased. Again I heard that sucking sound followed by, "I'll need a little help here." I turned around. Kyle's left leg had disappeared, and his right leg was at a weird non-supporting angle.

"I'm stuck."

I laughed and began to trudge back to him. "Now how did you do that?" I queried, expecting no response.

As I neared him, the streambed began to look different. It had a gray matte color and appeared to have a fine uniform grain. As I got within twenty feet of him, I, too, began to sink. Quickly, I dropped onto all fours to distribute my weight more evenly. This maneuver helped. I only sank to the tops of my elbows.

Slowly and carefully, I turned myself so that I was facing upstream with my feet pointing towards Kyle. Next, I tried to back up while keeping my weight evenly distributed over arms and knees.

As I got within reaching distance, I said, "Grab my feet."

When I felt his fingers tightly around my ankles, I started to move forward. Now we were both on all fours. Slowly we inched ahead until my left hand hit something hard. Instinctively, I grabbed it. As I raised it, mud ran down my arms and dripped in globs from my elbow.

As the mud fell away, I saw that I was holding a large,

toothy jaw. Still holding it high above my head, I said, "Look, Kyle. It's a jaw bone of a cow."

"Gawlee," was the long, slow reply, soon followed by "Look a here, Doc!"

I turned to see Kyle pointing to a white rib bone protruding from the clay at the edge of the stream. Then we spotted another and another. The area was strewn with the disarticulated carcass of a cow. We both began to laugh.

"Good thing no one is standing on the bank with a camera," Kyle said.

It took us several minutes to pass through the carcass of the cow and regain solid footing. The greenbrier-choked bank looked inviting after our trail through the belly of the beast.

After hauling ourselves out of the quagmire, we were able to get a better view of the whole scene. Huge chunks of bone littered a large clay pit. Now that the leaves and overburden had been removed, it was possible to make out a fifty-foot stretch of fine, gray clay strewn with bones.

"How many carcasses do you think there are?" he asked.

"Don't know," I said.

Then after a long pause he said, "Likened to be one or two more."

I'm Not Going to Tell My Mother

I WAS FORCED to take the spring semester off because being confined in a room with circulating diseases was deemed unwise for a person with a weakened immune system. I was hired by a contrite paper company to search their land holdings for diverse areas that might be worthy of preservation. This was not a volunteer gesture but a court ordered mandate for repeated destruction of wetlands and violations of water quality standards.

I was given a key to the metal gates, maps of the land holdings, and instructions to investigate all potentially significant areas. When filing my reports, I was to trace my trail of investigation on the maps provided and report only the most significant findings.

Many of the areas were bisected by streams and contained patches of upland hardwood forest. I soon found that the majority of the land holdings were covered with second and third growth pine plantations planted on old, eroded cotton fields. Clear-cutting followed by herbicidal spray was the common forestry practice for these areas. Once the weeds and native vegetation had been killed, a monoculture of improved Loblolly Pine was established. Such management practices on already degraded land resulted in even more soil lost to erosion.

TO A BOTANIST these areas were a depressing assortment of gullies populated by alien species, briers, blackberries, and deadfalls. It was hard getting into these holdings and even harder to follow one's progress on the maps provided.

The only reason I doggedly pursued this project was to stay active while I was going through chemotherapy. I could sprinkle field days throughout the week as long as I had several days of rest in between. It was necessary, however, to hire an assistant.

Thomas was one of my students who stopped by almost weekly to see how "Doc" was doing. He dreamed of being a marine biologist and had transferred to the main campus of the University of South Carolina to pursue his career. A stroke in his junior year shattered his hopes and forced him to return home, lose weight, and search for a new career goal.

Thomas came through this setback with grace and humor. "I know I'm not going to live a long life," he said, "but I'm going to make it a good one."

Thomas offered to go with me into the briers. At first, I was concerned about his heart. He assured me that he needed the exercise, and he would be fine.

He proved the perfect choice. Thomas could not read a map, didn't know one plant from the other, and had no eye for identifying sensitive areas. He was, fortunately, a quick learner. He always walked behind me so he could "see how Doc was doing." He was responsible for collecting specimens of significant plants for documentation.

Thomas was only five feet two and very black. If it were not for the white collecting bag he carried, I would have lost him on many occasions.

We traveled many a mile through some of the most eroded and alien weed patches I had ever seen. Often it would take us more time to find an access point than to survey the area. Most parcels were small landholdings surrounded by private land.

ONE DAY we were to investigate two small parcels lying along the eastern banks of Fairforest Creek. According to the map, there was an old public road that seemed to provide access to the downstream parcel. One glance at the road and we knew that access would have to be on foot. We parked our blue van on the east side of a county bridge, grabbed white bags, clipboard, hats, and maps, and set off in single file. The public road was little more than a four-wheel dirt track. It appeared to serve as an access road to an old, green, scum-choked fish hatchery. The ponds and the road were clearly marked on the 1964 topographic map.

The grass about the ponds had not been cut, but there were fresh tread marks on the road. They disappeared behind an eastward leaning shed at the edge of the clearing. The shed appeared to be filled with white buckets and old rusting machinery of uncertain age or use. The old fish ponds were now habitats for snakes. Slithering sounds were eerily common as we slowly picked our way between the ponds.

At the east edge of the clearing, we could make out three white slashes on a large Water Oak, the corner markings of the timber holdings. We made our way more rapidly, now that our destination was identified.

"Some of these snakes must be huge," I said.

Thomas said nothing but decreased the distance between us.

It was a cool morning in June. The forest we entered was lush and dark. Late spring flowers carpeted the forest floor. For weeks we had been walking a degraded landscape. Now finally, we had found a jewel of diversity. Orchids were in bloom, and the white flowers of Old Man's Beard dangled over our heads. Large patches of May-apple carpeted the lower woods, yellow now in the deepening shade of summer.

I picked a twig from an unusual looking understory shrub.

"Oh, that smells terrible," said Thomas.

"What?"

"I smell something — something like benzene."

I handed him the branch. "Take a whiff of the torn end of the branch."

"That's it," he said. "It smells really bad."

"Well, I'll be," I said. "This must be *Lindera benzoin*. I've never seen it with leaves this big or this far into the Piedmont. It's common in the mountains but not here."

"How did it get here?" Thomas asked.

"Well it probably once was found all up and down these rivers, but as the banks were clear-cut and disturbed, it died out. This is just a little refuge where it has been able to hang on. We've just stepped back into what used to be."

He took a sample and gently placed it in his bag.

It didn't take long for us to inventory the holding. It was quite small, just a small, low-lying woods on the south side of the creek, protected by a steep north-facing slope.

On the way out, we retraced our steps, disrupting many of the same snakes that we met on the way in.

As I approached the road, I was surprised to see a blue Mercedes Benz parked behind our van. A man in a suit was leaning on the hood of the car.

Thomas stopped. I went up to investigate.

"I'm Dr. Newberry, and this is Thomas, my assistant and student. We've been hired by the Champion Paper Company to identify floristically diverse areas on their properties."

"There are no Champion holdings around here," he said.

I took out the maps and pointed out the property that we had just visited.

"We were evaluating this small tract of land," I carefully explained.

"How did you get there?"

"We followed this road to the far end of the clearing where the Champion property begins. It's identified on the maps as an old public road." I again offered the map for review.

"This is not public land. This is private property. I would appreciate it if you're going to trespass, that you call me and request permission."

"I'm sorry for this mistake, but we had no way of knowing that this was private land. There are no 'No Trespassing' signs and no signs of recent activity. We saw no house or any indications that we were trespassing."

"Didn't you see that shed and the cut field?"

"Frankly, we were more concerned about the snakes."

"Well, in the future, I would appreciate it if you called me before you violate my rights again."

He handed me his business card. He was an engineer at a microchip plant about twenty miles to the north.

"We have to check a holding west of here this afternoon." I showed him the property on the map. "Do you have any suggestions as to how we can get to it?"

"They don't own that property," was the indignant reply.

Again I showed him the map that clearly delineated the parcel as Champion Tract 024.

Finally he said that I might be able to get into the acreage using a frontage road on the far west side of the property. "But you might not be able to get this van down that road. It's pretty washed out."

I thanked him, but indicated that if I couldn't get in using the frontage road, we would have to walk upstream to the site.

He grunted. "Well, next time you want on any of my property, give me the courtesy to call first and explain the exact nature of your business."

With that, he got into his blue Mercedes and drove off.

All the while this had been going on, Thomas had his head down and was quietly processing the specimens we had collected. I heard him put the press in the van, but now I couldn't see him.

I walked around to the back of the van. There he was hunkered down on the rear bumper.

"What was that all about?" Thomas queried.

"Beats me. He's an engineer at Monsanto. But what he was doing running up and down this country road at 11:30 in the morning is beyond me. He must live near here."

"Where's his house?"

We both looked around again. There was no driveway, no clearing, no sign of construction.

"Wonder what he's hiding around here?" I said to myself. "Well, let's get some lunch and rehydrate before we tackle the western acreage."

"He must be going to work. He had a tie and suit on," Thomas mused. "Or maybe he had come home for lunch."

"At 11:30? The Monsanto plant is twenty miles from here on county roads."

We ate quickly. All the while we looked for clues that might bring closure to the morning events.

"There's something he doesn't want us to find. So... let's get out of here. He told me of a frontage road we might use to get to the next site."

The directions were good, and we found the road with ease, but it was just as described. The ruts would have swallowed a VW Beetle. My Dodge Caravan was not engineered for serious ditch dodging.

"It looks like it will be easier to walk upstream from the bridge – and cooler, too."

Within minutes we were back at our old parking spot at the bridge.

I parked near the old road, being careful not to block the entrance. Leaving the car unlocked, we gathered bags, maps, and clipboards, and headed upstream.

The blackberry brambles were thick, and little progress was gained until we came across a dirt track that crossed the creek and proceeded in a sinuous curve in the direction of the desired patch of upland woods. Although arching thorny canes continued to grasp at every patch of exposed skin, the going was considerably easier than slogging up the creek.

Within twenty minutes we could see the white-slashed trees marking Champion land.

As WE SLIPPED THROUGH the last blackberry thicket, a cooling shade fell upon us. We were in the midst of a mature hardwood forest. The soil was spongy with deep piles of

Chestnut Oak leaves. Many of the trees were over two feet in diameter with straight branch-free trunks supporting egg-shaped canopies.

Thomas and I stopped and stared upwards, our mouths agape.

Quiet settled about us.

I kicked at the duff. The earth beneath our feet was deep, dark, and loamy.

"How old do you think these woods are?" Thomas asked.

"Maybe 100-150 years. Chestnut Oak is a slow growing tree that does well only in shade. It's been cut. See, here's an old stump. But that was a long time ago."

"I don't think I've ever been in a forest like this one," Thomas muttered.

"We might find some old American Chestnut sprigs growing from the roots of these old chestnuts humbled by the blight."

It did not take long before we were in the midst of a sea of chestnut saplings.

"There used to be a tree right here. See how the sprouts are in a ring? They are coming from buds at the base of an old chestnut trunk."

"That tree must have been five feet at its base," Thomas exclaimed.

"Maybe more."

"It was probably just too small a piece of land on too steep a slope and too isolated to bother with, or there might have been a land dispute preventing access. The tract was too small to warrant a court suit and too isolated to sell."

It was a tiny wood lot that had escaped the ravages of cotton, timber, and time.

The land across the creek, also owned by Champion, stood in stark contrast to our magical woods. It had been clear-cut and was now an unsightly collection of deadfalls and feral weeds. The land stood baking in the noonday sun. Heat rose off the acreage and hit us in waves whenever we neared the forest edges.

We spent two hours in this woodland. Outside of the chestnut sprouts, we found nothing rare, nothing that truly supported preservation. True, the trees were mature, and such forests are increasingly rare, but the area was small, with more edges than mass. Preservation would be almost impossible.

R<small>ELUCTANTLY</small>, <small>WE RETRACED OUR PATH</small> through the thickets of blackberry. As we stumbled out onto the road, I stopped abruptly. There, sitting on the top rail of the fence was a tall woman in her thirties dressed in a blue denim shirt and pants.

"I thought my husband told you not to trespass," she was almost yelling. "I can't believe that after he told you not to go onto our land, you would continue to defy him."

"I told your husband of our intentions, and he knew that we were going to investigate the Champion holdings west of the bridge."

"Did he not tell you to call and get permission first?"

"Yes, but I interpreted that to mean on future visits."

I looked over at Thomas. His eyes were as big as golf balls.

Twenty minutes later, I was apologizing for the misunderstanding and assuring her that we had completed our work in the area and would not be coming back.

"May I take you to your home?" I asked.

"No, that won't be necessary," was the curt reply.

Thomas slowly got into the car, making sure that he kept his head down and his eyes cast away from the fence.

She was still standing by the fence as we drove off.

"Well, that beat all," I said.

Thomas remained silent.

We had gotten less than a half mile north of Fairforest Creek when a county police car with his blue lights flashing approached us from the southbound lane and squealed to a halt in front of us.

The officer walked slowly to the car.

I rolled down my window.

"We had a report of trespassing down at the Golightlys' place."

I explained the survey and the access road that on the old maps was listed as a public road.

"Can I see your license?"

I was fishing for mine when I felt a tiny tap on my right arm. I turned towards Thomas. The golf balls were back. In his trembling hand was his South Carolina license.

He took both IDs and headed back to his car.

"How did he get here so fast?" I wondered. "We are not close to any police station, and we're in the least populated portion of the county."

We sat there, stunned and bewildered.

"It will be all right," I said to Thomas. It was a feeble attempt to reassure both of us.

The officer returned. "Well, everything checks out." He handed back both of the licenses. "The Golightlys have had some trouble down here, and they're a little skittish."

"If they're that worried, they need to post the property. There was no indication of any land ownership other than Champion."

"I'm going down to the Golightlys' now," he said.

I looked over at Thomas as I handed him his license. Beads of sweat were punctuating his forehead.

He looked back at me and in a whisper-cracked voice said, "I'm not going to tell my mother."

I laughed and replied, "I'm not going to tell mine, either."

Mind Over Metal

I'M NOT A MORNING PERSON. When I found myself in a small university in the Upstate of South Carolina teaching an 8:00 AM biology class, I tried to adjust. The only way of becoming mentally viable by eight was to get up at 6:13. With a pit stop at McDonald's for a large cup of coffee, I would get to school about 7:30. Several more cups of coffee and an established routine made most things possible.

Invariably, as the semester progressed, problems arose. One particular morning I had absent-mindedly misplaced my notes. Normally this was not too much of a problem, but this particular lecture required overheads. Winging a lecture without overheads would be much harder.

As 8:00 approached, I became more and more frantic. No overhead transparencies, no time, no way!

The housekeeping crew usually cleaned the carpets between seven and eight, before classes began. They were running late that morning, too, and were just getting to my office area. I noted the loops of vacuum cleaner cord at the threshold of my office and jumped over them as I dashed into my office for one more frantic look. At that instant Mabel, who was vacuuming, yanked the cord.

As ankle met cord, the adrenaline-generated energy was transferred to a forward toppling motion. My right forehead took all the impact as it collided with the metal doorframe.

Down I went, out cold!

As I came to, I was aware of something or someone trying to right the situation.

Our geologist, a well-endowed man with muscles honed by boulders, had me under the arms and was attempting to lift me. A warm trickle was running down my forehead and collecting in my left ear.

I mumbled, "No, no, not yet, Lyle."

Lyle eased me down.

At that moment Phil, our stockroom assistant, and a very serious young man, came around the corner and stopped at my feet.

"Doc, you're bleeding," he blurted, and ran to get the medical kit.

Moments later he returned, lugging the medical kit that had been mounted on the wall of the stockroom.

"I'm not very good at this, Doc," he apologized.

"That's OK," I encouraged. "Are there any gauze pads?" I asked.

"Yes."

"Any tape?"

"Yep."

"Well, put a pad over the cut and tightly wrap it with tape."

Phil gave me a rather oversized pad, and I held it while he mastered the tape. Tight was an understatement. My eyes were squished into squints, and the tape circled my head like a fallen halo.

Another student had been sent to tell my class not to leave. I'd be a bit late.

The tight bandage made seeing a challenge. My hair was plastered tightly to my head and pushed up into a lopsided beehive.

As I got uncertainly to my feet, I spied my notes on the floor under my desk. I grabbed them, and off I went to lecture.

"Don't leave. Doc's out cold, but she'll be here soon," was scribbled on the board.

This cryptic note had been heeded. Not a student had left. Curiosity is a wonderful attention grabber.

This was a very young freshman class. I didn't want to spring a leak in front of them. Being left-handed and right brow beaten, I could sort of turn halfway to the board. In this position I could write on the board, and my body shielded the brow from the direct gaze of the class. If a gusher came I could catch it before the class knew.

Phil's efforts worked well, and the blood was not forthcoming.

I gradually worked myself into full lecture mode. As the hour progressed, I became aware of a steadily increasing pressure headache, but until the very end, the concentration required to weave a lecture together kept the pain at subconscious levels.

As I gathered my goodies together at the end of class, the head of the biology department appeared at the door. He informed me I was going to the doctor.

"But I'm not bleeding, and I have too much to do," I replied.

"I don't care," he replied. "I will take you, or you can take yourself, but you are going."

I was escorted off by a friend. She had already told the doctor we were on the way. The wound opened up again in the doctor's office. This shortened the wait. Two hours and fourteen stitches later, I was back at school. My halo was gone, and so were several crucial tufts of hair.

The wound healed, and the semester passed without further incident. I had almost forgotten the whole bloody mess when I happened upon a student evaluation. It read, "She really knocks herself out for her students."

The Mud Puppy and the Bride

ONE SUMMER I was inventorying all known populations of the endangered plant *Sagittaria fasciculata* (known to almost no one as Bunched Arrowhead). This rare plant grows in seeps in Greenville County, South Carolina, and Henderson County, North Carolina, and nowhere else in the world.

These mud-filled springheads act like sponges swelling during periods of wet weather and gradually shrinking during droughts. As a result they help to regulate the water flow in upcountry streams.

During this study I realized that the large seeps on the Furman University campus were being heavily overgrown, severely reducing the flowering potential of the Bunched Arrowhead plants. Weeding appeared to be the only option.

The only problem was that the mud suspension did not support even a diminutive botanist — and my diminutive years were long past.

The only method that seemed to work was to use the four pedal approach. Crawling through the mud on my hands and knees allowed me to sink only about a foot into the quagmire. Using this method I could propel myself through the mud, liberate the weeds from the mud, and toss them onto the raised seep edge.

The mud was cool, and I rather enjoyed the mud bath until I reached a section filled with dead holly leaves. These spiny leaves punched through the skin giving an unwanted stimulation to the experience.

By the time I had weeded about one hundred square feet of seep, I was covered with a tannish ooze.

Fortunately, the seep drained into a clear, rocky bottomed stream. I chose a large flat rock in midstream and began my sponge bath. Soon there was a growing plume of muddy water filling the stream below my rocky perch.

Suddenly, I became aware that I was not alone.

I looked up.

On the top of the riverbank was a wedding party. They were lined up in all their whiteness and were quietly staring down at me and my mud plume.

No one moved and no one spoke.

I just gave them a small muddy wave and went back to my demudding.

I glanced up a few times, and they were still there. But as I did not remove anything but my outermost layers, they grew bored and returned to their celebration at the nearby picnic shelter.

To get back to my car, I had to walk past the party.

I gave them a wide berth as I drip-dried my way back to the parking lot.

Again, no one spoke. Sometimes there just aren't any words.

E-I-E-I-O

How can you use the dictionary if you don't know if the word begins with an "S" or a "C," "Ph" or "F," "P" or "N"? Believe me, I've tried. Bad spellers' dictionaries don't help, either. They only make matters worse, giving me spellings even I wouldn't have concocted.

It's been a humiliating battle all my life. Weeks have been spent on a report, only to have it come back looking like it had been dipped in the Red Sea. Papers submitted for publication have been editorialized out of existence.

Spell checkers help, but frequently, the computer can't even figure out what I'm trying to say.

I don't go anywhere without an electronic spell checker. Even if I'm just leaving a note, I'll use the electronic gizmo just to be sure.

My spelling gets worse under pressure. My physics professor once took forty points off a major test for misspellings. He promised to return the points if I spelled fewer than nine words wrong on the final exam. This was long before the handheld checkers. I was more worried about the spelling than I was about the test questions.

When the card came with my grade, there was a cryptic note at the bottom. "Eight words misspelled."

My students ask if I take off for spelling. I can't. I have no idea if it's right or wrong. But I warn them, "You can't just start off with the correct letter and attach a few humps ending with a straight line. It has to be phonetically correct."

Several years ago a student solved a part of the problem. "Doc," she said, "you don't have a problem with the consonants; it's just the vowels."

She's right, but I don't know how to fix it.

The humiliation and mental I.Q. lowering has had its positive side. It has made me a better teacher. I know the struggle and effort it has taken me to be semi-literate. It's a rare individual who doesn't come across some course or some discipline that is hard for him in college. Try as they might, for some individuals, science is like pulling a log-filled wagon uphill through mud. I am more sympathetic to their problems and try to approach the subject in several different ways so that these struggling students might find some leverage.

I Still Remember

ONE DOWNSIDE of field trips is the lock-step fashion by which students follow the leader through the woods. They don't want to miss anything. On many trips I feel like a bantam hen being followed by a new clutch of chicks.

This works fairly well most of the time — that is, until nature calls. You look longingly for a large tree and saunter over to it, only to be followed by fifteen or twenty students.

Men have it easier. They can pretend to check a strange plant or inspect the bark of a tree, but women tend to disappear from view. The students quickly become restless.

On a field trip to the mountains several years ago, I was desperate. I was cursing that second cup of coffee I had drunk at McDonald's that morning. The trip was nearing the end, and we were closing in on the van. The students were strung out in a line. Deftly, I migrated slowly to the rear. I stopped and let the last stragglers round a curve. Quickly, I darted into a low and heavily vegetated patch and sought relief, more concerned with not being spotted than with what I was squatting on.

An old still had been dismantled at this very spot. The sudden warmth on the metal set up a series of noisy clangs and bangs as the metal suddenly expanded, echoing like gunshots around the bend. The field trip participants ran back to see what had happened. There I was in a patch of poison ivy, my pants at my knees, and metallic rumbling still coming from the area around my feet.

"I guess I found a still," was all I could lamely reply.

This was several years ago. The students have all graduated. But whenever I happen to see one of them, he always says, "Do you remember that field trip when you found the still?"

I still do.

The Perfect Student

WHEN a master teacher dreams
It is of a student supreme.
A questioner in a conscious stream
A synthesis of a thought-out theme.

> A mind focused and camera ready
> But not a regurgitator of facts paraded.
> A questioner of the dogma stated
> A critical evaluator of facts dictated.

>> A student who is so situated
>> Makes connections never stated.
>> Who understands mathematical fractions
>> And works with self-motivated action.

A student who no excuse imparts
When things degrade to pieces and parts.
Who has responsibility for actions taken
That realizes failure is of his making.

> An assignment given is an assignment done
> On time and with references — some
> Rewritten, spell checked, and craftily spun
> One who discovers that learning's fun.

The dream a nightmare become
When there are students — none.
For a class to be a success
There must be more students, not less.

Excuses, Excuses

I'VE LOST my keys; I've overslept; I've lost my car in the parking lot at Walmart; I've just plain forgotten. But these reasons are just not good enough, so excuses are made.

We've all done it; some of us are better at it than others. After teaching for many years at a small university, I thought I had heard them all.

"My grandfather died, and I couldn't make it to the test." I heard that three times in one semester from one student. When I confronted him with my suspicion, I found out that it was true. The boy was from a family where there had been a number of marriages. He actually had two more grandparents to go!

The more outlandish the excuse, the more likely it will be true.

"Sorry, Doc, I didn't make the lab test yesterday; my boob busted." I was searching for a response when the middle-aged redhead continued, "but it don't matter. I'm not married any more."

"Sorry, Doc, but a deer ran through my hood on the way to school yesterday. He got his foot stuck in the engine, and I couldn't see to drive."

The student looked fine. No scratches, no bruises. So I asked him how the deer was.

"He will be delicious," was the reply. This is strictly illegal, of course, but I let it go.

EXCUSES SEEM to be a way of life today. My students will spend more time thinking of reasons why they couldn't get the genetics problems done than it would have taken to get an **A** on the project. Perhaps there should be a course on creative excuse making and a follow-up course on how to know when you've been had.

When the next student comes up with the distinctive floor surveying expression and begins the conversation with, "I'm sorry, Doc, but..." maybe I should just hand him a list of my favorite fifteen excuses and ask him to pick a number. It certainly would be more efficient. The number would go in the grade book instead of the grade, as sort of a ...fibber factor.

The suggestion list might go something like this:

1. *My boob busted — still my favorite.*
2. *My sports car (red, of course) caught on fire.*
3. *I kissed my girlfriend (boyfriend) too long this morning.*
4. *I can't write because I have ringworm.*
5. *My brother ran over our puppy, and he was so upset (pick dog or brother).*
6. *My books were stolen with my car and burned in the accident with the police car.*
7. *I let Billy Joe borrow my notes, and his phone is disconnected.*
8. *My dog ate my notes.*
9. *It was so hot last night that I studied in a tub of cold water. My notes fell in and all the words ran off the page. Guess I shouldn't have used washable ink.*
10. *I dropped my notes in the pigpen while I was doing my chores, and I can't stand to study them.*
11. *I have to work forty to sixty hours a week in order to afford to go to school full time.*

12. *I had colic.*

13. *I worked late at the library last night and put my notes on top of my car when I went to unlock it. They're somewhere between here and Simpsonville (forty miles of interstate away). Of course, it was raining at the time.*

14. *My sister gave my notes to her ex-boyfriend George who is in the class. (Of course, George is in a different section with another professor.)*

15. *I had to rush Mama to the hospital. She got one of her spells.*

One enterprising athlete failed to show up for a lab test. Lab tests require extensive set up time and need to be taken down immediately so other classes can be held. When he showed up three days later, I asked him the reason for his absence. I knew that the team had been in the regional finals the day before the test. Having been at the game, I knew my student had not played. No make-up was given.

Prospective medical students are very prone to excuses. The high GPA required for entrance into medical school fosters all sorts of deviant behavior. Several years ago I had in my class a young man who wanted to be a doctor. He worked weekends in the ER of a small hospital. The following week he always came down with whatever disease he happened to have seen in the emergency room.

After several semesters his grades were not good, and I sat him down in my office to discuss the reality of the situation. His GPA was 2.01. No medical school was going to look seriously at this young man. For most medical schools, the cut-off is 3.3 or even 3.5. He had taken so many courses that raising his GPA to even a 3.0 was statistically impossible.

I explained all this to him, but he looked optimistic. "I know several doctors who will give me great recommendations." And he continued, "My dad is a good friend of the dean of the _____ Medical School."

Finally, in desperation I said to the young man, "Son, the

only way you could get into medical school is as a cadaver."

His eyes lit up, and he became very animated. "That's great, Doc; do you really mean it?"

Now I was staring at the floor. "No," I said quietly. "But there are good jobs in EMS and Physician's Assistants programs that may be more in line with your academic record."

Hoping Is Coping

AFTER MANY YEARS as a college professor, I have heard the word "hope" used in vain too many times. It is always in reference to the same thing — a grade or an upcoming or past test or assignment.

"I hope you'll be lenient with us, Doc."

"I hope you're in a good mood when you grade this."

"Hope you grade on a curve."

I should respond, "I hope you have organized your weekend to give the topic the attention it requires," but I never say it.

The students see hope as a means of getting by and not as a way to truly succeed. It is so for all of us.

I am no different. I hope to get through the next meeting, the next lecture, the next week. I hope to do better next time. Like my students, I am hoping to get by.

But hope should be more than that. We can hope for the best, cope with the least, and demand that with each try the results will be better than the last.

The presence of a future is meaningless without hope. If conditions never improve, if change is not an option, then we are without hope. To live in such a world would be the cruelest of fates.

Hope is a physical need. Tomorrow and the future could not live without it.

For the sick it is the hope of getting better.

For the weak there is the hope of becoming stronger.

For the **F** student, there is the hope of getting a **D**.

And for the university professor, there is the hope of spring vacation.

PONDERINGS

Reflections

AT THE EDGE of the lake there is an azalea bush in full bloom. Actually there are two; only one is real; the other is a reflection. Yet on a still, bright day, both appear as twins mirrored in the lake's surface. Only one will feed the pollinator and bear the fruit. Only one will bend with the wind. The other will break — first into patches of color and then fade into gray.

Today, however, in the stillness the real and the imaginary are as inseparable as yang and yin.

If I were a pollinator, I would be confused and be drowned in the illusion of a perfect reflection. But nothing perfect lasts, and the reflection will shatter into zigzags of color when a cat's paw passes.

Sitting here on the dam with my back to the sun, a melding occurs. The fractured points of light reform, and the image becomes one with the real, only to be broken again by a duck's wake or a falling leaf.

Few things are as easily defined as a bush or its reflection. Even fewer ideas have a clear line of delineation. Absolutes are as illusory as the watery azalea. What is the cause? What is the effect? These are simple questions which are rarely answered with a single response.

In reality there is no one answer but a synergy of reasons, a cacophony of causes and effects.

That's what's so strange about the azalea and its reflection. It does not reflect the complexity of life but only the complexity of form. No insect will be fooled. No pollinator will drown in a futile attempt to pollinate the reflection, for the insect is not attracted by a single beacon but by a combination of attractants — smell, shape, color, and pattern.

We are determined to fail as scientists, as investigators, if we continue to look for the single answer. There is not one but many contributing factors. There rarely is one cause and rarely one effect.

Reflections mesmerize and lure us into a false reality. They transport us to a simpler world of right and wrong, true and false, good and evil. Perhaps this is the essence of the enjoyment of such a transcendental scene.

The Ides

I AM IN THE ABYSS where two seasons are at war. A cold drizzle — part rain, part mist, and part cloud — has South Carolina in its grip. Drops form on the still dormant branches, bow them with their collective weight, and coalesce into mega-drops which cascade onto the ground beneath. The moist air magnifies sound. Undampened by the nude branches, the random cadences intensify with the deepening of the fog.

Everything is in hiatus. Only the foreign yard weeds and the Bradford Pears are tricked into believing it is spring. The native plants are not fooled. They are still in tight bud. Aging botanists once fooled in their youth are wise to the falseness of an early March spring in western South Carolina.

The calendar is right; spring is still two weeks away. It's too early to plant, too early to weed, too early to wash the windows. It is the lull between the seasons.

Even the fireplace flames dance with a subdued glow. A small fire is all that is needed to beat back the dampness. The slow burning logs flicker and sizzle with steam. Small flames of red-orange with bases of blue dart and spar at the edges of the damp oak logs. They flare up into forked tongues that leap and crisscross before subsiding into a column of smoke. The flames, too, are in a war with the wet and the cold.

As the fire dies, the coals begin to resemble the shape of an alligator's head with ember red eyes and a gaping glowing mouth. The few flames that remain are flickering through blackened fangs. The ferociousness is fleeting. It dies like the March wind with the coming of spring.

I should go prepare a new lecture; I should finish my taxes; I should clean my desk of all those almost completed projects; I should read something... be productive... start something new. But my mind is on the flames. Which of these sparring tongues will last the longest? Which will win the battle for the log? After all, there is a whole new season coming with plenty of unfilled hours to get all those tasks done. But if I don't just sit here — and watch very carefully — I will never know which flame won.

The dog seems to sense the importance of this moment. She crawls up onto my lap facing the fire. Instinctively, I cradle her head in my hand. We both stare into the flames. It is the Ides of March, and deep down it doesn't matter which flame wins. In truth, it is not so much the end that is important; it is how well the fight is waged. This looks like it's going to be an especially good one. I can't leave just now.

The Best Part of the Day

I HATE an alarm clock. It is the abrupt shift from sleep to the uncertainty of the new day that disturbs me. It is the sudden awareness of all the jobs that need to be done, all the problems left unsolved, all the broken things that need fixing, and all the ominous suspicions of machinery about to fail that frazzle me into consciousness. This wave of minutia overwhelms me in that microsecond between oblivion and the start of a new day. It tires me before I even have a chance to get out of bed.

However, there are those luscious mornings when awareness comes on slowly. There is time to curl into a ball wrapped in well-warmed sheets and let the consciousness of the new day slowly overtake you. Gradually, the plans for the new day unfold. I might ease into the day by turning on the weather channel and with that information in place, slowly plan the day. Will it be yard work, lecture preparation, fieldwork, or that book waiting on the coffee table? Or will it be a day of rejuvenation, a day when nothing is planned? I could lie here in this suspended state all day, but I never have.

The best alternative is to make a cup of coffee and curl up with the dogs on the couch. I am mesmerized by the swirling patterns of cream in coffee. The battle between the dark and the light serves as an allegory to my fight to focus on the jobs ahead. The house is quiet. The morning light plays off the leaves of the trees framed by the glass doors opposite the couch. It is a luxury just to sit and do nothing, to think of nothing, to worry about nothing.

If I am lucky, I can keep this feeling for an hour or so before the day crashes in, and problem solving begins. Once that threshold is crossed, there is no returning to the couch and reclaiming that peace.

But if I am really lucky, and make it back to bed in the evening before I'm too tired to care, there is a chance for that feeling to return. After all those cold corners have been conquered and the lumps arranged properly, there is a melding of body and bed. The mind empties, and the relaxed feeling makes me one with the covers. My body seems to flow into all those cozy corners, and I drift slowly back through that oblivion zone into sleep.

Southern Greens

IN SPRING all plant life is woven into a green mosaic shag carpet which cloaks the Appalachian Mountains. There are only subtle differences in hue during the din of a thunderstorm. But intense contrasting colors appear in the first rays of sun following a spring shower. Linguistically, all of them fall under the canopy of green.

No color is so varied. None has the capacity to produce such inner calm.

The front porch of a mountain cabin may be the single most important factor in increasing the longevity of Carolinians. The view mesmerizes, calms, and satiates the soul. The scene is reassuringly constant and at the same time in constant flux. The changes are the result of the melding of the hour of the day and the season of the year. Such a synergism produces a kaleidoscopic panorama.

Psychologists must have done studies on human emotional responses to color. I don't need to read the literature. I can feel the calming effect of a green hillside in spring. I know the éclair-like delight that begins in the sternum and radiates outward. Expanding upward, it creates an unconscious uplift of the corners of the mouth, ignites a sparkle in the eye, and a surge of endorphins in the brain.

As a botanist I could go into detail concerning photosynthesis and its powering the energy requirements of all life. But I won't.

Today I'm more interested in the emotional power of green. I am content to sit on the porch and watch the parade, to marvel at the changes, and be content just to marvel at the display. I will not ask the usual scientific questions: how? why? or what if? Today is a day to just let it be — green.

                PINE
              LIMES
          MOSS, IVY
        LODEN, SAGE
        MINT, GRASS
       OLIVE, APPLE
     JUNGLE, SPRING
    FOREST, HEATHER
   EMERALD, VERDANT
  SEA FOAM, OLIVE DRAB
LIGHT GREEN, BLUE GREEN
YELLOW GREEN, GRAY GREEN
             DARK
            GREEN

The Murmuring Pines and the Hemlocks

SEVERAL YEARS AGO, more several than I would like to count, I read an account of logging operations in northern Wisconsin at the turn of the twentieth century. One statement still stands out after all these years. Early in the account the authors stated, "Anything under two feet in diameter was left in the woods as it was not worth the effort to process it."

Yesterday I was stopped behind a lumber truck. No single log was greater than fourteen inches at the base. The diameter at the skyward end was smaller than a woman's forearm.

If Paul Bunyan were to walk into our forests today, he would never take the ax off his shoulders.

Several biologists have made the dire prediction that we will be the last generation to know the forest primeval. As our collective memories fade, so too, will our desire to see a diverse growth of mature hardwoods.

But on a hot summer day in South Carolina, even the shade of the scrawniest pine tree is sought after in a parking lot. Old neighborhoods with shaded sidewalks provide cool power walking zones. Old cemeteries with majestic, open-grown oaks provide shaded environs for meditation and reflection on the past.

Single grown oaks can still stir our senses and create in us an appreciation of grace and elegance. Every time I drive south to Atlanta, it has become a ritual to look for the majestic, old, lonesome oak that still grows in the median just south of the South Carolina–Georgia line. As I pass it, I breathe a sigh of relief. Over the years I have seen it decked with yellow ribbons, black ribbons, and with bows. It's not just me that is stirred by the elegance of this tree. Somehow it connects us all with what is good, right, and ethical in this world.

What is it that causes such a response? Is it a primal knowledge that this life form was here before us and could long outlive us, is it the towering majesty of the massive trunk, or is it the juxtaposition of symmetry of a perfectly grown tree casting a long historic shadow on a major artery of the modern South?

If a single tree with its symmetric splendor can stir contentment, a mature diverse forest must produce an even more intense sense of oneness. The cooling shade, the aesthetic arch of branch and bough, the smell of the woods after a rain, the graceful pattern of trunk and branch against the splashes of sun and the deep shade — all have a soothing effect on our souls.

When there was more forest than open land, the wilderness was something to be feared. It was an entity that needed to be beaten back and conquered. When traveling by stagecoach through dense forests in the eighteenth and nineteenth centuries, it was traditional for women to draw the curtains in order to wall off the wild. Now that the wilderness and the primeval forests are almost gone, our souls cry out at the loss.

When will we realize that we are playing God with our futures and the futures of all life forms on this planet?

When man felled the last tree on Easter Island, he forever changed the diversity, productivity, and livability of that small rock in a Pacific sea. The scenario is only taking a bit longer on all the larger chunks of rock dominated by man. The scenario will be the same.

The Saming of the South

SOUTH CAROLINA has changed. It has been an imperceptibly slow change that is only now having major repercussions. No longer is there a localized style of life. The adults shop at Walmart, and the teenagers choose the mall. We eat bagels and wash them down with designer cups of coffee. We even give them a proper name: Latte, Cappuccino, and Cafe Mocha.

In 1976 when I moved to the mountain side of South Carolina from the hinterlands of Wisconsin, I was stepping into a different culture.

The suddenness of this change hit me when I went to do my first grocery shopping. A blazing white display of Dukes Mayonnaise covered a huge span of shelves. Peas and beans came in every color and size and were piled on one side of an endless isle. There were pinto beans, black-eyed peas, navy beans, large lima beans, baby limas, great northerns, red kidney beans, speckled beans, split peas in two colors, small red beans, and lentils. In the produce department there were not just green beans, but pole beans, crowder peas, snap beans and, oh, so many more. To a Wisconsinite peas came in two forms, canned or frozen. They were always green and usually preceded by the word "English."

Greens were yet another puzzle. Collards, kale, and all their cousins were unheard of in the North in 1976. Spinach was the only green produce in Wisconsin back then.

When I went to buy bagels and cheese, however, the cupboard was bare. I went by the cheese counter twice before I noticed it. Cheese was available as long as it was Velveeta. The grocer had never heard of Colby, Monterrey Jack, or even cheese curds. No sausages, no knockwurst, bratwurst, liverwurst and no good hot dogs were to be had. What made a wurst lover even more distraught was the lack of a good beer to wash it down.

Bread came in one shape — rectangular — and the color was always white. Rye was a rarity and pumpernickel an impossibility.

The meat aisle was an adventure. There were parts of organisms I had never heard of before — chitlins, cracklings, fatback, tripe, and gizzard, just to name a few.

Eating out was only beginning to become a common recreation. All restaurants had ads like — "Home Cooking." I guess this was so you might think nothing had changed.

But the North moved south with me. Now we have fresh bagels and lox, and Italian, Mexican, German, and Thai

restaurants that advertise authentic cuisine.

But there are subtler changes such as the names of streets. Roads used to be named for the person who lived at the end of them or for some characteristic about that particular way. Names like Mill, Mud Pit, Stone, Stoney Pebble, Cudd, and Golightly Lane are disappearing, replaced by names such as Done Roaming Lane, Almost Heaven Drive, Set Awhile Circle, or Camelot Acres.

People don't wave at you when you pass them in a car any more. Drivers no long stop to let a funeral pass. When you smile at a stranger he usually gives you a questioning look before reluctantly returning the favor.

Most people sense that the pace is faster. To me, the pace has always been brisk, but it just took the Southerner a little longer to tell you how to get lost.

Perhaps that has been the problem all along. The Southerner may have always had the answer, but by the time he got the words out, no one was listening.

Cycles of Change

AT THE BEGINNING of the year, our local television station went to a new weather reporting format. It tells of weather fronts approaching in six shades of green. Snowstorms are coded in shades of gray with varying speeds of falling flakes. All this frontal parade is superimposed over a neon-colored map of the southeastern United States. The camera can zoom in on a single major intersection or pan out to show the entire east coast buffeted by a raging Gulf Stream. I can only imagine what sensory overload will befall us during hurricane season.

There is a problem, however. It is now mid-February, and they have yet to get a single forecast totally correct. The precision of the predictions has not changed. It's boundless and the flare limitless, but the information is no more correct than it ever was. The errors just look better.

Everything is advertised as new and improved. The fine print tells us that the pattern on the box has changed so that smaller boxes appear bigger. What has changed is the packaging, not the contents.

We now seem to be yearning for old boxes. Americans did not lose their love for the squared off, boxy cars. When Detroit and Japan went to the new rounded models, we fell in love with the squarest boxes on wheels — the Jeep Cherokee, the Rav 4 and the Humvee.

With the retrofitting of America, we have seen the return of the Volkswagen Beetle and hiphuggers.

We hear of the decline of today's moral values and SAT

scores. In dismay we have turned from the larger and larger unpersonalized classrooms and have begun to teach our children ourselves. Homeschooling works. It has for years. The one-room school is now found at the family kitchen table.

We fear that our social structure and culture are in decline.

No high culture survives forever.

Changes have all come before and will all come again. The driving forces for such change remain the same: famine, pestilence, war, strife, and the birth of a new hope.

Thoughts on a Sunday Afternoon

SUCCESS is a concept we all feel we understand. But do we? Biologically, success is easily explained. For a species, success is living long enough to reproduce. Once offspring have been produced, success becomes the progeny's problem.

The most successful organism living today is the cockroach. Roaches were scurrying under the feet of dinosaurs and are still in a hurry. Today their terrain is a bit different. Now it's our kitchens, bathrooms, breadboxes, and garbage dumps. Next time you swat a roach, you might consider that you are swatting at the picture of success.

But to modern man, a cockroach is not seen in such a light. We define success in more cold, metallic terms: two cars in the garage, a $60,000 dollar a year job, a 50-inch TV screen, and a gross gross national product.

Why bring all this up? Why question such an elusive concept as success?

To me this may be the quintessential question, a question whose answer, if there is one, may determine the success of the human species. Our present dominance on the face of the earth is causing us ever-increasing problems.

Modern medicine has sustained life and produced an ever-increasing number of people living on the food chain long after their reproductive years are over. This is a great ecological burden. I do not advocate the alternative, however.

Modern machines have alleviated a lot of drudgery of day-to-day life. The result is a growing population of out-of-shape people, people that must spend their ever-increasing free time exercising to hone muscles that our modern machines no longer keep in tone.

Free time produced by the discovery of transistors, the computer, the cell phone, and the four-cycle engine is a boon to man. We fill that time, however, with endless movies, computer games, and other electronic time wasters.

Homo sapiens is the dominant species on the face of the earth, the climax species of the ecosystem, but our consumptive waste is threatening the stability of the whole planet.

To the credit of the cockroach, it never invented the computer chip or the garbage dump. The roach has never forgotten its place in the environmental chain of events. It is preprogrammed by instinct and is never confused by facts that need to be interpreted. It simply knows what it knows. The rest is unimportant. We, in turn, must learn the hard way, from our mistakes. Intelligence may not be all that it is cracked up to be.

Next time you pass a pile of garbage, remember that the roach has successfully adapted to that environment, too.

Success may have to be redefined by modern man. A workable definition that is more in tune with the environment must be developed. Then, and only then, may we take our place with the roach in the garbage piles of the future.

The Drought

Humbled by humidity
Blistered by the heat
It seems to take an eternity
For the sun to retreat.

The horizon casts an orange glow
That descends upon the land
It's reflected in the water flow
That seeps where it once ran.

The lengthening shadows of the pine
Prostrate upon the ground
Radiate to the ends of time
Where only dark abounds.

While overhead a soaring cloud
Teases the parched to think
That rain and lightning clouts
Will offer all a drink.

The stillness is oppressive
The clouds continue to build
The silent world is pensive
With hopes of pools to fill.

Shadows merge with the dark
The coming of a breeze
Ruffles the feathers of a lark
And moves the leaves of trees.

Somewhere there is a rain
Offering evaporative relief
Water drops on windowpanes
And runs along a leaf.

Huge water drops — a Rorschach blot —
Are spread across the clay
Irregularly lobed and brightly bold
Sharp contrast to dust and gray.

The margins of the blots converge
But there's not enough to meet
The sun has come; the clouds diverge
No chance for heat relief.

The drought that holds us in its dust
That cracks and crazes the land
The leaves all cloaked in a crust
That is not green but brown.

El Nino is the reason
That's what the weathermen say
There's been no rain this season
There will be no rain today.

No rain tomorrow either
No fronts to come next week
No arctic lows or cold fronts bold
To offer long-term relief.

Eternity is before us
There is no end is sight
The heat is all that is discussed
Community baths tonight?

A Trace of Rain

A splat or a plop
It depends on the drop
A rill or a run
It's how fast it comes.

A gain and a loss
The drops crisscross.
No route is the same
On the trails left by rain.

The dust of the morn
In rivulets is born
To be etched into paths
Not destined to last.

Water entropy inspired
Has washed away mire.
With gravity and slope
The cleaning is rote.

But with rain clouds gone
The paths won't last long.
New dust coats soon come
It's the price paid for sun.

BASEBALL

It starts in the spring
And continues through fall
By September the parks ring
With the best of baseball.

A baseball diamond's a wonderful place
It's beautiful, serene, and sculptured with grace.
Made of crisp, sharp lines of white, brown, and green.
All magnified on a huge TV screen.

There are green-checkered fields and fresh watered grounds
White chalked lines and fresh raked mounds.
There are bright painted placards and walls full of ads
And new caps and bats and glove-handed lads

The glories of summer fade into fall
That's when it's the best for us all.
Brush backs, balks, strikes, and past balls
All are a part of the game of baseball.

Power and glory and individual grace
Statistics and tactics all have their place.
But it's control in the game and a steady pace
That will see a team through a long pennant race.

A game with no clocks and no time limit
The subtle excitement is there every minute.
Bloopers, line drives, and arching fly balls
Safe or out — it's all in the call.

Send him or hold him or ask him to take
The decisions depend on what is at stake.
Inside, outside, or thrown high and tight
The game is composed of finesse and of might.

A batter who hits safely one third of the time
Is a hero, a champion — a wonderful find.
Where else in the world can you be a success
When you are productive one third of the time or less?

Ode to a Tomato Sandwich

JUICE LEAKS from the edges and oozes through the bread. Seeds drizzle from one's mouth and slip down one's chin. On the palate a complex flavor sensation unfolds. Bitter and sweet, salt and sour combine with a soothing moisture and a slippery texture to produce an uncanny culinary experience.

It's summertime in the South. It's a time for shrub-ripened tomatoes to flood the market. It's tomato sandwich time in South Carolina.

The North may envision summer in the South with images of magnolias, mint juleps, and lazy evenings on the veranda. But for most people of the South, summer is envisioned in a tomato sandwich.

Southerners are a little bit more tolerant of variations on the treat of the sandwich than they used to be. Butter is reluctantly permitted in the place of mayo. Cheese and salami are also allowed, and the bread can be sourdough. But pure Southern tradition requires white bread slathered with Duke's Mayonnaise piled high with fresh, blood-red tomato slices. The mayonnaise must be so thick that when one takes a bite, at least half of the tomato slices shoot out the other side. Salt may be added upon request.

To wash down this taste sensation, a true Southerner will require sweet tea. Not hot tea, not unsweetened tea, not tea with artificial sweetener, but brewed tea sweetened to the saturation point with cane sugar. It is tea so thick that an ice cube cannot sink. It is a tincture of tea with the taste of sugar water.

Grits in the morning — tomato sandwiches for lunch. You can't get more Southern than that, and who would want to? There is a lot of heaven to be found between the lily white bread slices of a tomato sandwich.

Comfort Food

Peanut butter, popcorn, potatoes, and dips
Oodles of fried things, gravies, and grits
Hot dogs, corn dogs, wursts, and brats
Cookies, candies, doughnuts, and tarts

Fast food, soul food, and crisp chicken skin
All have combined to create the state that I'm in.
Mouth watering treats that stick to the waist
Saturated fats all add to the taste.

> My arteries are clogged
> My colon runs slow
> My heart beats as fast
> As a human heart can go.

>> My waist is widening
>> My blue jeans are tight
>> My figure is keeping
>> My toes out of sight.

>>> If only I could live
>>> On raw carrot sticks
>>> My middle might not
>>> Have become quite as thick.

Salads, veggies, and herbal teas sound
Like a diet designed to keep me around.
But what is the pleasure in such a life
No desserts, no treats — just eating right?

Where is the joy and the comfort to be
When your diet is always 100% fat-free?
Where is the solace, where is the gain
When you always partake of a diet — plain?

Celery and cheese that's fat-free
Is just not the stuff for a person like me.
Food is my recreation; food is my vice
It's not just a thing to sustain me for life.

    The fat's in my hand
    My foot's in the ground
    But there's a smile on my face
    As long as I'm around.

The Dilemma Facing Middle America

I DO NOT ENJOY vacations. I'm usually very careful to plan more than twice the amount of work that can possibly be done during the time off. Always I return to work tired, and out of sorts, and in need of another vacation.

During the fall semester this year, the administration decided to cut expenses and close the university for the month of January; thus, I was faced with a six-week vacation with very little time to form contingency plans.

Then the ad came. Generally when a multi-colored brochure comes announcing, "Mr. Newberry, you and your wife may have already won a trip to Afghanistan, a Mercedes-Benz hub cap, and a rechargeable screwdriver, or a personalized mongoose," I use it to start the next fire in my wood stove. I used to laugh at the assumptions that Gillian was a male name and therefore, if I owned my own home, I must be married with a wife, two kids, a dog named Spot, and two cars in the garage. I hardly notice any more. All these assumptions, of course, are wrong. My dog is brown and named Crumb-licker. I drive an aging white truck, and I live in a log cabin.

But alas, this ad was more convincing than most. It listed five individuals who had claimed their TV and one lonely name whose TV was as yet unclaimed. That someone was Mr. Gillian Newberry.

I like TV about as much as I like vacations. I have on

more than one occasion gotten so mad with myself about the time I have wasted watching hours of programs whose plots I cannot remember the next day that I have sold the set. There is such an unclean feeling about having wasted a whole weekend, month, or millennium with only an electric bill and a worn-out select button to show for all the effort.

The timing of the ad was impeccable. The next weekend was New Year's. I was expecting a house full of people with no TV to keep the kids busy. It would be great if they would busy themselves watching the endless parades and the football follies. Actually, I sort of wanted to watch the games myself.

Having a day free and seeing an easy way to alleviate the problem, I made an appointment to pick up the twelve-inch black-and-white set.

Arriving early, I toured the area of Elk Droppings, a North Carolina ski resort for an exclusive group of people. A more artificial community would be hard to imagine. There was no Sears, Walmart, or Dollar Store, no shoe stores, or appliance repair shops. America did not shop here. The town was made up of real estate offices, ski shops, gas stations, and liquor stores.

I was sure that an elk had never placed a deposit here, or if so, it was a final act on the way out of town.

Construction was going on everywhere. It was hard to imagine that the country was in a deep recession, for this small mountain community was metastasizing at an alarming rate. Stick-built condominiums and timeshares were being built on every slope that was less than twenty degrees.

It was impossible to miss my destination. A one-hundred-foot sign advertising the wilderness retreat on Lump Mountain in garish green, blue, and orange marked the reception area. The building itself was painted a rustic brown. Looking more closely, I realized that only the front façade was brown; the back remained unpainted.

As I stepped into the reception area, an overworked young lady asked me a few brief questions. She seemed very uninterested in the answers. Camouflaged in this conversation were questions concerning my debt, marital status, spouse's occupation, and recreational pursuits.

The important portion of these preliminaries was the filling out of a form.

QUESTION 1: Where did you spend your last vacation?
MY ANSWER: *I've never really had one.*

QUESTION 2: Where would you like to spend your next vacation?
MY ANSWER: *The Arctic, Greenland, or the Galapagos Islands*

QUESTION 3: Occupation?
MY ANSWER: *Biology Professor*

QUESTION 4: What is your salary?
MY ANSWER: *I could not remember. I was sure it was over the minimum required.*

After a two-hour wait, they piled us into a carpeted school bus, drove us around the community of Elk Droppings, and showed us the neighboring town of Sliding Slope.

This tour was a bit different from the one I had taken earlier. Much of the construction centered around exclusive country clubs. We toured them all. One of these came complete with a small airstrip so that private planes might land and park for the few hours it takes to play eighteen holes of golf. I think a parking lot was also part of the plan.

The developers' names, famous to all but me, were dropped as if they were personal friends.

"Why, Jack plans to live here, and Arnie is looking forward to playing on this course when it opens."

The roar of bulldozers and the rhythm of hammers were heard everywhere.

Looking briefly at a wandering mountain stream, I spied a clump of Watercress. How long is that patch going to last before it ends up in an executive salad served at Jack or Arnold's country club? There is some hope for that lowly clump. Perhaps no one but me knows it is edible, at least not in that form.

The bus turned and started up a gravel road. The road led past a guardhouse and began to climb to the top of Lump Mountain. As we ascended, we passed through seas of new condo units — condos to the left of us, condos to the right of us, condos above us, and condos below us — all of them on the sale block. All were newly built with freshly graveled drives, pruned vegetation, and all the wooden areas freshly painted.

I tried to visualize the area in five or ten years — the roofs in need of repair, the road rutted, and the paint mildewed. These changes would not take long in such a rugged mountain area.

The timeshares at the very top of the mountain were our destination. Here on a terraced slope were perched one hundred salt-boxes tied together in lines, as if this construction could combat the winds of October. The view was magnificent. All of the trees had been cut so that every window had an expansive view. From every bed one could imagine the sight of buzzards soaring into a crystal clear sky.

Every apartment had potted geraniums. Each pot held geraniums of a common hue and hung from exactly the same window. The tour took us through single, double, and triple bedroom units. Each had built-in everything. Our final destination was the newly opened year-round pool.

My glasses fogged. As they slowly cleared, I took a closer look at the bottom of the pool. "Is that a vinyl lining?" I asked.

"Yes. Isn't it beautiful?" was the smiling reply.

"How long will that last?" I muttered.

The lady next to me answered, "About five years. Then the sand beneath it will shift, and it will have to be redone."

"That figures."

The walls in this hot house were paneled; the panels had already begun to warp.

Finally, they herded us into a big room, and we were

offered wine from paper casks and minute cheese bits on bread crumbs.

"Conservation, at last," I thought.

Each prospective buyer was assigned an agent. We were seated facing a board telling us that "ten lucky people" had signed up today. Only forty more of the one hundred units were still available during the ski season, and these would cost more tomorrow.

As it was probably obvious at this point that I was not a prime client, I was escorted into a small room to see a videotape of how timesharing works. Soon a very nice, well-dressed, black couple joined me. We had gotten to know each other on the bus.

We sat in the dark watching the seven-minute tape. It was in color, of course. As the picture cleared, a very attractive setting emerged. A very professional gentleman was sitting at a desk surrounded by leather-bound volumes that he would never read.

He began to speak, "Middle America is faced with a very critical problem —" He punctuated this statement with a long pause. Finally, he continued, "— how to spend the ever increasing amount of free time."

I turned to my friends next to me. "I wonder how the third world would react to that statement?"

They nodded and smiled.

Serious problem? You are faced with a critical decision. The answer was to buy into the country club life. HELP! I am trapped in the consumer's quest to spend and the entrepreneur's quest for a quick buck.

If this is the good life, please give me the TV, and let me return to my log cabin.

As it turned out, they were out of TVs, but I could have a twenty-piece set of matching burlap bags with genuine vinyl trim and matching name tags.

"No," I said. "I am interested only in the TV."

"No problem," was the reply. "We will send it in twenty to thirty days."

This did not solve my New Year's problem.

I descended from the mountain sure that I would never see the TV and secretly hoped I wouldn't.

I have rented a color one for the weekend. It will go back on Monday. I will go back to my wood stove and my stereo assured that I am more content than most of the middle Americans faced with the dilemma of how to spend their free time.

My Mother's Hand

THE LIGHT had turned red; I eased off the gas and cruised to a stop. Yet another love song wafted from the radio.

Not another lament to unrequited love! Was there nothing else to sing about? I reached for the knob to search for an alternative when my eyes fell upon my hand.

WHAT THE HELL!

How did that happen? Just yesterday, the skin was spotless, tight, and pliable. Now the skin was crazed like a raisin. Veins stuck out like tributaries of the Amazon. There were more brown spots than on the cheeks of a redhead. These were so numerous that they mimicked a tan. The knuckles resembled elephant knees and the nails were more ridged than a Ruffles potato chip.

I raised my hand in amazement.

The image was unmistakable. It was my mother's hand.

But when? How? Only yesterday that hand had clutched a comforter, written a thesis, made lesson plans, signed a mortgage, and buried a parent.

Now it told a different story. The numerous white scars reminded me of past skirmishes with paring knives and glass shards. The knobby knuckles, wrinkles, and splotches only foretold the debilitating future.

It was a hand that recorded past history, and it foretold the future. It is a future as tremulous as the last strains of a love song.

The Doc in the Box

GOING to the doctor has never been an uplifting experience. The task requires a realization that you may not be able to fight through an illness without some help.

But waiting hours in a doctor's office with a bunch of sick people has never been appealing. There is always the possibility that you will leave sicker than when you arrived.

After weeks of a nagging earache that extended through my jaw, I gave in and went to one of these walk-in clinics — a Doc in the Box.

She took my height, weight, and blood pressure. So far — no surprises. Then she asked if I had a general practitioner.

I said, "No. I have been using the walk-in clinics for several years."

She looked at my chart. "You are seventy-one years old; you have diabetes, and you're obese."

Wait a minute. I knew I was seventy-one, but I had not gained any weight and last time I checked the weight charts I was well down in the overweight column.

"Doc, I'm still one hundred and fifty-six pounds, and I'm five feet one inch tall."

"No, you are only four foot nine, and that puts you in the obese category. You need to get more exercise."

"I go to the gym four times a week. Walk my dogs a mile and a half each day. No, I don't need more exercise. I just need to find those lost four inches."

Postscript

THIS effort would not have come to completion without the help of many of my friends. Eva Pratt typed and retyped, proofed and reproofed the stories. Diane Cantrell and Melissa Pilgrim edited and caught numerous typing and spelling errors. Janie Marlow offered her expertise on formatting and guided the book to completion. My mongrels added a lick or two and lots of hair and accompanied me on many meditative walks and pondering strolls about our pond.

List of Plates

HOME
Page 7, Old sharecropper's house that was near the last turn for home. It was a beacon that meant my journeys were almost done. With that turn I could feel my heart rate slow, my sanctuary from the work-a-day-world was at hand.

Page 16, Dwarf-flower Heartleaf (*Hexastylis naniflora*) grows with Mountain Laurel on north facing slopes near streams in Greenville and Spartanburg Counties in South Carolina and nowhere else in the world. My students and I have searched many slopes in search of this federally threatened species.

Page 19, Organ Pipe Mud Dauber.

Page 20, Organ Pipe nests of the Organ Pipe Mud Dauber on rafters of a mountain cabin.

Page 30, Florida Scrub Jay that landed on my hand when offered a peanut.

Page 39, Reflection of the Grand Tetons in the waters of Jackson Lake.

HOUND TALES
Page 59, Griffin before haircut.

Page 60, Fleabags, alias Crumb-licker, alias Coco.

Page 67, Riley, named for Walter O'Reilly of M*A*S*H. They had many characteristics in common.

Page 70, MacDuff.

Page 73, Black Molly.

Page 75, Griffin after haircut.

Page 76, Sassafras.

TALES AND TRAILS OF A BOTANY PROFESSOR
Page 85, Students holding up peanuts to attract wild Florida Scrub Jays.

Page 98, Blackberry Lily (*Belamcanda chinensis, Iris domestica*) found on rock outcrop, Union County, South Carolina.

Page 116, Bunched Arrowhead (*Sagittaria fasciculata*). This rare plant grows in seeps in Greenville County, South Carolina, and Henderson County, North Carolina, and nowhere else in the world.

Ponderings

Page 129, A pig in paradise, a contented pig having just engorged a huge pile of pancakes. The Bahamians placed the pigs on an uninhabited island in the Bahamas. Tourists flock to the island to feed the pigs. The pig population has grown, and the porkers have learned to swim out to meet the manna-carrying tourists. In the fall the fattest pigs are a protein treat for the natives.

Page 141, A South Carolina garage dressed up for a barbecue.

Postscript

Page 165, Hairy, a mongrel who was hit by a car and came to die in my carport. He had every worm known to find an internal home in dogs. I took him to the vet's where he was cured of all known infestations. He became the most grateful of my ditch dogs.

Front Cover

Blackberry Lily (*see note above, re page 98*).

Pig (*see note above, re page 129*).

A hand of Bananaquits. These wild Bananaquits were attracted to a hand dusted with sugar. The picture was taken at the ranger station on the Exuma Islands in the Bahamas. The hand feeding of the birds is no longer allowed.

Back Cover

Students discovering a large population of the federally threatened species, Dwarf-flower Heartleaf.

Griffin was found wandering the schoolyard of the Day School in Spartanburg, South Carolina. He dearly loves children and was named after their school mascot.

Oconee Bells (*Shortia galacifolia*) is an endangered plant species that is part of the unique flora of the gorges about Lake Jocassee in Pickens County, South Carolina. Preservation of this species was required before the dam forming the lake could be constructed.

Made in the USA
Columbia, SC
07 November 2021